# 1
# this
# is a
# book

this
is a
book
about games

this
is a
book
about
games
for people

this is a
book about
games for
people who are
interested in
learning about a
new type of play
that lets people
be supportive,
cooperative and
open with each
other

this is a
book about
games for
people who are
interested in
learning about a
new type of play
that lets people
be supportive,
cooperative and
open with each
other, and that
means everybody

this is a book about games for people who are interested in learning about a new type of play that lets people be supportive and cooperative and open with each other, and that includes everybody, especially people who need to defrost their refrigerators.

this is a book about games for people who are interested in learning about a new type of play that lets people be supportive and coopera- tive and open with each other, and that includes everybody, especially people who need to defrost their refrigerators and people who would like to use the games and ideas in this book to make situations they are in more playful — for example, playing with your family, students, colleagues at the office, gym class, scout troup, campers, street gang, and consciousness-raising group, at your p.t.a. meeting, kiwanis club dinner, synagogue, senior citizens center, bridge club, y.m.c.a., faculty meeting, office party, church picnic, and sons of the desert convention, not to mention lovers on a cruise, cheerleaders on a bus, divorced parents with custody for the week- end, friends at a party, or alone by yourself in your apartment, and who could forget using these games at a friend's wedding reception, sitting around the passenger lounge at the airport after your plane has been de- layed, during the break time at a particularly boring lecture, riding in a car with your family, or sitting on the bench at a softball game waiting for your turn at bat . . .

7

everybody's
guide to
noncompetitive
play

# playfair

by **matt**
**weinstein &**
**joel goodman**

***Impact*** 🦪 ***Publishers***
POST OFFICE BOX 1094
SAN LUIS OBISPO, CALIFORNIA 93406

# dedication

To the PLAYFAIR tribe — Pamela Kekich, Bill Perrotta, Jerry Ewen, Bill Fritz, Joanna Jeronimo, Jeanie Cochran, and all the sisters and brothers who will join with them. Your passion for people, your vision of the way things can be, and your determination to make a difference in the way we all live our lives is a gift to everybody ... and especially to me. What a life!

M.W.

To Mike Michaelson, Gene Borgida, Karen Krug, Janis Cromer, Eliot Pfanstiehl, Patti Bourexis, Bruce Stanley, and Dorcas Miller — Here's to all the playful and powerful times we have shared in the past 15 years! I really cherish our long-standing, loving, caring friendships, and look forward to 120 more years of spontaneous laughter, cooperation, playfulness, and joy as we work to fulfill our dreams.

J.G.

Copyright © 1980
by Matt Weinstein and Joel Goodman

Design Copyright © 1980
by Joan Stoliar

Library of Congress Cataloging in Publication Data

Weinstein, Matt.
   Playfair, everybody's guide to noncompetitive
play.

   1.  Games.  I.  Goodman, Joel B., 1948-
II.  Title.  III.  Title:  Noncompetitive play.
GV1201.W437        793            80-12591
ISBN 0-915166-50-X

Design by Joan Stoliar, New York, New York
Typography by Dexter and Magee, San Luis Obispo, California
Cover photo by Charles West, Oakland, California
Other photo credits, page 249.
Printed in the United States of America

Seventh Printing, February, 1988

Published by
*Impact* Publishers
POST OFFICE BOX 1094
SAN LUIS OBISPO, CALIFORNIA 93406

# what is playfair?

**an idea:**
> People come together in games which are cooperative, where everyone wins, where no one loses, where the goal is pure fun, recreation, and relationship. . .

**an event:**
> A playtime on college campuses, at business conventions, at schools, in community groups, churches, temples, service clubs, families. . .

**a way of life:**
> Developing attitudes of cooperation in play — instead of playing competitively to win — helps people to live more cooperatively in all their daily activities . . .

**a source of fun:**
> From the PLAYFAIR experience — idea or event or way of life — people can get more fun out of living. . .

> . . .and now. . .

**a book:**
> Conveying the spirit of PLAYFAIR through words and pictures offers **everyone** a chance to play. . .an invitation to learn hundreds of skills, games, and practical ideas that you can use in your life and work.

# contents

# 1 an introduction to fun and games     1

# 2 why are we so serious about play?    20

- unlearning to play
- competition and self-concept
- the spectator sports syndrome
- competition and relationships
- is competition always bad?
- PLAYFAIR: a model of cooperative play
- playfair: a resource book for players
- some tips on how to use this book
- the PLAYFAIR recipe

# 3 a playful sample (how to throw a great party!)     38

- incorporations
- imaginary ball toss
- moonwalk
- the human spring
- off balance
- brussels sprouts
- standing ovation
- big wind blows
- crescendo
- wonderful circle

# 4 mixer games: breaking the ice     60

- introductions
- moving name game
- singing name game
- birthdays
- animals
- hum-dinger
- chorale of the vowels
- human treasure hunt

**5** intimate and family games: the fun begins at home     **78**

- wrist dancing
- finger dancing
- pleasant memories of childhood play
- how to start an argument
- rebound
- songs by syllables
- bouncing the person
- floating on the ocean
- flying back stretch
- octopus massage
- i love ya honey, but i just can't make ya smile

**6** energizers: what to do when your meetings start at 7:30 sharp and end at 10:30 dull     **104**

- four up
- the 39 steps
- back to back dancing
- amoeba tag
- train station
- groupwalk
- roll playing
- simultaneous songs
- group cheer

**7** learning games: recess always was the best part of school     **124**

- quick shuffle
- 1-2-3-4!
- boss, i can't come to work today
- open fist simulation
- clay-dough
- emotional relay race
- human tableaux
- picture charades
- mutual storytelling

**8** mind games: why is a half-defrosted steak like an impulsive idea?    144

•safari
•mind reading
•name circles
•either-or metaphors

**9** games for leadership training and organizational development    160

•three positions
•stop and go
•five changes
•touch blue
•elbow fruit hop
•the cargo cult

**10** endings: when you come to the end of a perfect play    178

•highlights with punctuation
•massage train
•wiggle handshake

**11** how to invent your own games    186

•recycling old games
•starting from scratch

# 12 answers to your questions about play                    204

- cooperation in the "real world"
- working with competition-oriented groups
- applications to the office
- applications to coaching
- characteristics of a play facilitator
- guidelines for sequencing games
- good party games
- sensitivity to physical differences
- developing a sense of community
- does this really work with adults?
- play sessions for children and adults together
- shy people
- possibilities

# 13 a value-able look at play                    220

- are you someone who . . .?
- rank ordering
- alternatives search
- clarifying questions

# 14 resources                    232

- joel goodman
- matt weinstein
- PLAYFAIR
- sagamore institute
- the humor project
- pamela kekich
- bernie de koven
- the games preserve
- the new games foundation
- jeffrey mc kay
- marta harrison
- re-evaluation counseling
- clifford knapp
- ymca
- david and roger johnson
- contact improvisation
- inter-action

# alphabetical index of games                    247

# photo credits                    249

# 2 why are we so serious

This book is written for people who want to have fun, and people who want to develop a new way of relating to their families and friends, as well as for teachers and therapists and parents and youth counselors and other people with a "professional" interest in helping people to play cooperatively together.

Once you begin to think about it, there are an enormous number of opportunities for play. If you're willing, and open, you'll often find an occasion (and an available audience of prospective playmates) to use the games in this book. The next time you're together with a group of people and you feel even the slightest bit bored or alienated, take a moment to fantasize to yourself what that group of people might look like if they were playing games. We have found that people are *almost always* ready to have some fun, anywhere and anytime—they're just waiting for "permission" to do so. As soon as you announce, "Hey, let's all play a game while we're waiting!" you give them that permission (and the structure) to come alive in a dead situation. By being the catalyst for this "guerilla playfare," by giving people an invitation to play with you and the other people around them, you can touch people's lives wherever you go. All of life can be our playground if we allow it to be!

# about play?

## unlearning to play

When a group of people get together to play, no matter how well-intentioned they may be at the start, they're probably going to wind up playing together the way that they've always been taught to play together—competitively and unsupportively, with a strong focus on individual heroics.

We believe that is not the *natural* way to play . . . it's just the way that everybody has been *taught* to play. So if a group of people want to get together and play together in a noncompetitive and supportive way, first they're going to have to "learn" how to do it. And that means that someone is going to have to "teach" them how to do it. And that someone could be *you*.

It's not that difficult! In fact, it's great fun. Don't get nervous if you've never done it before—that's what this book is all about. Noncompetitive play is a new experience for most people, and it needs to be structured in a way that allows the players the easiest transition away from their competitive conditioning. This book will provide you with dozens of different alternative ways to help people do just that.

## competition and self-concept

Most people have learned that the way to be a standout in games is by putting other players down, by boosting themselves up at everyone else's expense. In volleyball, when someone misses a simple shot, everyone leaps on him[1] with "Oh, great shot!" or "What's the matter, your feet nailed to the ground?" or "Why don't you try to hit it with your head next time?"

---

[1] The problem of combatting the sexist use of language is one for which many possible solutions have been proposed, none of which we are crazy about. Our solution is to play around with a number of different possibilities — sometimes we use "s/he", sometimes we say "him", sometimes "her", sometimes "he or she" — we're going to try to be as random as possible!

21

Many of us have been rewarded in the past for putting each other down in our play: the person who says the most clever put-down statement, who gets the biggest laugh at someone else's expense, is the person who is admired in her instant of glory. It's the way most of us have been taught to play, and even though we may *understand* that that kind of behavior is inappropriate for supportive, noncompetitive play, those phrases may come to our lips in moments of excitement anyway.

Most games, as they are played today, at best ignore the development of self-confidence, and at worst destroy self-confidence. There are too many people who do not feel good about themselves as playful people. Many people learn early in life that ''to the victor belongs the spoils.'' Victory has become the dominating force in the way people play—and for many people, it has spoiled play altogether. Vince Lombardi's popularization of the ''winning is everything'' philosophy has led to the emergence of winning as our new national religion.[2] It's gotten to the point where Billy Martin, while managing the New York Yankees to the World Championship of professional baseball, declared ''it's not how you win . . . it's just winning that is the name of the game.''[3]

Winning can be wonderful . . . if you always win. But there is a flip side to that, which is the flop side of self-confidence—there are usually more non-winners than winners. In fact, our current overemphasis on winning is making us a nation of losers (of self-confidence).

George Leonard suggests that ''far from releasing physical aggression, the traditional approach (to games and playing) is likely to *teach* physical aggression.''[4] We would add that traditional games teach *verbal* aggression as well. And this aggression does a great deal of violence to people's self-confidence and to their ability to see themselves as playful.

Joel was working and playing with a group of thirty junior high school students recently, and he asked them to make a list of the put-down statements that are a regular part of their vocabulary. In just five minutes, they were able to generate 200 different insulting phrases that are an everyday part of their lives! In a climate where put-down statements are the norm, players soon begin finding fault with their own performances, as well as those of other players, and they soon begin to make self-deprecating statements (sometimes aloud, sometimes only inside). The danger in all this is that they may begin to *believe*

---

[2]George Leonard, ''Winning Isn't Everything—It's Nothing,'' *Intellectual Digest*, October 1973, pp. 45-47.

[3]Quoted in AP story on June 26, 1977.

[4]George Leonard, ''Physical Education for Life,'' *Today's Education,* September-October 1975, pp. 74-76.

these self-put-downs, and many even incorporate them into their own self-concepts:

"I'm a klutz."

"I'm a bird brain."

"I'm not coordinated."

"I better not play, 'cause everybody will laugh at me."

"They're always going to choose me last."

Under attack from an increasing number of put-down statements, the person will often surrender, and retire from playing. The psycho-logic goes something like this: "If I'm always getting put-down when I play, then it doesn't make sense for me to keep on playing—I'd rather quit." This can even happen to people who see themselves as playful:

Some people have stopped playing in their lives. They don't run around at all, they don't do anything, just because they're not "good enough" to compete. I know that when I was in high school and we were first learning the trampoline, I didn't participate right away. By the time I got up enough nerve to try it, I was a couple of weeks behind everybody else — and they could do fancy flips — and I was ashamed to admit that I had to learn the basics. And, so I never did. The gap just got wider and wider and wider until it was absolutely impossible because of peer pressure for me to ever get up on the trampoline ... there would be hoots of derision for the beginner to get up there, when the more polished people could just get up there and put on a show.[5]

One of the advantages of establishing noncompetitive play structures is that they can provide special training grounds where the players can practice interacting and speaking supportively and appreciatively to each other . . . . And then the players can begin to extend this type of supportive verbal interaction out into the other parts of their lives. If the pressure to "win" at all costs is removed, then the urge to verbally humiliate other players soon disappears as well.

# the spectator sports syndrome

It is startling how early in life this "spectator sports" syndrome starts. A recent Surgeon General's survey posed the question to mothers of first graders: "Suppose there wasn't any TV—what do you think your child would do with the time

[5]Matt Weinstein, in Joel Goodman and Clifford Knapp, *Completing the Environment With People: A Guidebook for Leading Nature and Human Nature Activities,* (in press, 1980).

23

now spent watching it?" Ninety percent of the mothers responded that their children would be playing.[6] Studies show that children spend 15-30 hours per week in front of the television, compared with only about two hours in planned physical activity.[7] These young play "drop-outs" quickly grow up to be arm-chair quarterbacks and Monday night football widows. We wouldn't be surprised to find a carry-over into other aspects of life as well. In many ways, we are turning into a spectator society, filled with voices that tell us, "I can't fight city hall," "my vote doesn't mean anything," "let someone else do it," "they could do it better than I," "what do I have to contribute?" Democracy was never meant to be a spectator sport!

The noncompetitive approach to playing can "detoxify" some of these negative aspects of competitive group play. People can come to regard playfulness with celebration rather than distaste. Players who don't feel excluded and judged (judged that they "fail," that is!) continue playing for the rest of their lives. We want to help people feel good about themselves as they actively participate in their own recreation. We hope to help channel our society's orientation from "instant replay" to "instant we-play"!

# competition and relationships

The principal difficulty with competitive games is that they prevent the players from developing a true sense of "connected-ness" with each other. All human beings experience a need to belong, to be *a part of*, rather than *apart from*, the group. Feeling a part of a group is the first step in active part-icipation.

Games are like a language—they have incredible potential for helping people to make contact with one another, to connect with one another. Unfortunately, many traditional games lose out on this opportunity—or even squelch it—because they provoke competitive interaction among the players. Competition can lead to exclusion, the antithesis of connection, belonging, inclusion. Beyond that, competition can breed a "killer" instinct, destroying both confidence and community. Competitive structures and rules often seem to bring out the "worst" in people . . . it's a Dr. Jekyll/Tan Your Hide transformation. When we place more importance on rules than on people, we are in bondage to competition, and lose sight of our common human bonds.

---

[6]Marie Winn, "TV Stunts Creativity in Play," *The Saratogian,* February 21, 1977, p. 6A.

[7]Alan Haas, "Is Your Child in Good Physical Condition?" *Family Weekly,* November 6, 1977, pp. 16-17.

# is competition always bad?

We believe that competition in and of itself is not bad. What *is* bad is what people allow competition to do to themselves and to others. We agree with George Leonard, who says "there is nothing wrong with competition in the proper proportion. Like a little salt, it adds zest to the game and to life itself. But when the seasoning is mistaken for the substance, only sickness can follow."[8]

In 1977, as part of the research for this book, we designed a survey to examine people's ideas and histories of playfulness.[9] The survey consisted of seventeen questions, such as: "(#2) Who was your favorite playmate when you were younger? What made this person your favorite? Describe your "ideal" playmate as a young person—what qualities would you have looked for?" and "(#4) What is a good experience you have had playing as an adult? What made it a positive experience for you?" and "(#9) With whom are you most playful? What is it about that person that invites you to be playful?".

---

[8]George Leonard, "Winning Isn't Everything—It's Nothing," *Intellectual Digest*, pp. 45-47.

[9]See Chapter 13 for a full list of the questions included in this survey. We have included a sampling of responses to this survey throughout the book.

Participants in the survey were permitted to leave blank any question they could not or would not answer. But there was one question that no one left blank: "(#5) Can you remember a painful play experience you've had? Describe it." Almost all of these responses had to do with competition, with a "painful" experience involving success and failure and being judged by one's playmates. Here are some representative samples:

Back when I was in the fifth grade, it was very clear that boys played baseball, dodgeball, and football. The girls' domain was jump rope, dolls, and tetherball. One day, our gym teacher forced all of us to play tetherball — this was bad enough in itself ... but to top it off I ended up playing against Suzanne Parker (who had a crush on me at that time ... and she proceeded to "crush" me in the game). I was humiliated, since it was very gauche at that time to "lose to a girl," and I took a merciless ribbing from my friends. In looking back on this incident now, it is painful for me to see the sexism and rank-outs that were rampant. And would you believe, I haven't played tetherball since that fateful day.

In swimming class, we were being tested on our diving ability. There was a new instructor from a different YWCA, and I just could not do the dive to her satisfaction. I kept climbing up to the diving board over and over again, tearfully feeling humiliated that it wasn't working out.

Trying to make the baseball team that all my friends were already on ... I sat on the bench for a couple of weeks and finally the coach sent me to second base. To start the game, the catcher throws the ball to the second baseman. He threw it and I missed it — and I was taken out of the game before it even started.

Many people don't even consider playing anymore, because they equate play with exclusion and being left out, and feeling like a "loser." There is a need to create cooperative models of playing together, in order to provide a balance to the competition which envelops us. Without cooperative alternatives from which to choose, we really are at a loss in deciding when competition is an appropriate mode.

Cooperation can leave people feeling more "together" (literally and figuratively). It can help us develop a sense of connection with other human beings. In a classroom, in an office, in a team, in a family ... we believe that people who play together really will stay together. Cooperation can lead to a feeling of "playing with people" as opposed to "playing against people."

We can change the rules by which we play—by which we play games, as well as the game of life. It could be as simple as saying to a student who has missed school, "Let's try to catch you up with what we've been doing so that you can feel part of the group." It could be having a group collectively build a snow sculpture (rather than giving awards for the individual "best" sculpture). It could be following the example set by the professional baseball player who literally "put his money where his mouth is":

A Montreal amateur baseball group is $5,000 richer Thursday because controversial relief pitcher Mike Marshall earlier refused the $5,000 cash award that accompanied his selection as the Montreal Expos 1973 Player of the Year. Marshall was chosen as the Expos' top player by the Montreal chapter of the Baseball Writers' Association of America. But at a presentation ceremony here six weeks ago, Marshall refused the $5,000 check on the grounds that he refused to compete against his teammates for money. He later presented a letter to the sponsoring company further explaining his stand.[10]

---

*Perhaps we should add "play" to the list of common human needs — so much energy could be used in play instead of turned inward or outward in a negative way.* [11]

---

[10]AP, "Friends Receive Marshall's Prize," December 14, 1973.

[11]You'll find responses to the Playfair survey displayed like this throughout the book.

# PLAYFAIR: a model for cooperative play

We are excited about the use of play and games to explore with people what a truly cooperative society might look like. Our vision of the world is that people are *naturally* cooperative, joyful, and playful beings, but that many of us have been *taught* to act otherwise. There aren't enough models of what a supportive, play-filled lifestyle might look like, and that's what we are trying to offer with our play-workshops across the country, which we call PLAYFAIRS.

One of the most important things about the games in this book is that they can be used as tools to help create a sense of community among the players, in much the same way as we have been able to do at our large-scale PLAYFAIR events. Although we have worked with groups as large as 3500 people at a time, there is no minimum or maximum number of people that is the "right" size for a cooperative play experience. You may be playing with five other people or five hundred other people—through a cooperative play experience it is possible to create a sense of united purpose, of connection to others, of belonging.

There is a very real need in this country for the community-building experiences that a noncompetitive play session can provide. Most of our work as play-consultants has been with groups of people who have an ongoing relationship and who wish to develop a stronger sense of community—groups like the freshman class of a university, an office staff at a large corporation, the participants in a senior citizens' mobile lunch program. And this longing for a sense of community is not limited to ongoing groups—people gathering together for the first time at a party can also benefit from the "instant community" that a cooperative play session can provide.

Shortly after a PLAYFAIR event at the University of California at Berkeley, Matt and psychologist-friend Dale Larson discussed the virtues of PLAYFAIR as they jogged together. Matt recognized the value of Dr. Larson's insights, and asked him to hold the thought until they could get it down on tape. They sprinted over to a pay telephone and called Matt's answering machine. What follows is a transcript of that call:

DALE LARSON: What I see PLAYFAIR doing is providing an experience of community that's lacking in the society generally. People don't have an opportunity to be with each other outside of their prescribed social roles. And in PLAYFAIR there's a unique opportunity to do just that: to be yourself, to be spontaneous, to feel that you can interact with people in a safe context, and explore different self-expressions and different facets of

yourself without having to be constantly "on guard" . . . Which is the average person's normal state of consciousness and being, being on guard and worrying that people will not be positive, not be accepting, not be understanding.

In PLAYFAIR, you don't have to be on guard, and it creates a unique context which can, I think, make a dent in the need for the experience of community. It can decrease the amount of alienation that people feel. People don't really feel "connected", there isn't a meaningful contact for most people with each other in their everyday lives. In PLAYFAIR you're seeing yourself in a new way, you're seeing people outside their social roles . . . it's supportive, it's fun, it's positive in the feeling tone of it.

And the reason it's so successful a program *now* is because there's such a desperate need in the culture for it right now. You could go back to other periods in time and try to do PLAYFAIR and people wouldn't respond to it, they'd just say, "Hey, that's the way life usually is." But our whole technological society is very fragmented. The community of the neighborhood, the community that was provided by the church, the community that was provided by the family, all are disintegrating around us . . . you have a real strong need for some kind of sense of psychological community.

In this fragmented world the major problem of the time is demoralization. You don't have the kind of social support system that people used to have and that's so important, and it contributes to stress — you're on guard all the time, you're looking and you're not finding, you're not getting confirmed and appreciated by other people. And that's why coming together in a PLAYFAIR is a real liberating experience. So it's exhilarating to do it, even if it's only an ephemeral, one-time experience . . . because it can be a model of the type of community that we want to build in the rest of the world.

Obviously, PLAYFAIRS are just the beginning of an exploration of the way things can be. Up until now most people have felt that they never had a choice about the way they lived their lives. There has been only one alternative — go out there and *win,* and too bad if lots of people have to lose. Through this book, we want to say to people, "You don't have to live like that, you have real choices in your life. Take the cooperative spirit of what we've created here and make it happen in your life everyday!"

We think it can happen. And we hope this book can help it to happen.

# playfair: a resource book for players

The playful activities collected in this book have been successful in helping to create a play community in which people are full of high-spirited, joyful feelings about themselves and their playmates. These games are designed to help create a play situation where the players don't feel a need to put each other down, but rather begin to feel nourished and supported and valued by those with whom they are playing. To create such an atmosphere of trust, support, and good feelings among players with a strong history of competitive conditioning (which includes most everybody!), an introductory noncompetitive play experience has to be a smoothly structured and facilitated one. That means that the first few games need a strong and confident leader.

The instructions for these playful activities are written from the point of view of a leader giving an introductory noncompetitive play experience to a group of adult players. All of the activities are followed by "comments," intended to give the play-leader further insight into the structure of the games, how to lead them, and how to sequence them.

Incidentally, when you're reading "Directions to the Players" you'll come across three dots . . . from time to time.

The dots mean that the play leader should pause for a few moments, usually to allow the players to complete a step in the game.

Most of the activities in the following chapters are taken from PLAYFAIR, a noncompetitive play experience that is designed primarily for adults.[12] We have written the instructions for the games as though we were working with a group of adults, because most of you (readers) are adults, and will be playing the games over in your head as you read along. However, teachers, parents, recreation leaders, camp counselors, and child therapists who are looking for games and activities to use with your students, clients, and children — DON'T PANIC! You've come to the right place! Most of the activities in the following chapters are also directly applicable for use with young persons. In some cases, the games need modifications if they are to be played with young people, and we've tried to include the help you'll need to adapt the games to fit your own group(s) in the "comments" section following particular games.

Of course, none of the instructions for the games are intended to be reproduced verbatim. Each of you has your own specific group with whom you will be working, and your own unique style of presentation. If you find yourself *reading* these instructions aloud to a group, you

know that you must be doing something wrong! Party-giver, parent, teacher, therapist, recreation leader—whoever you are—these games are meant to be modified, mangled, and molded into something just right for your specific needs. Take them as a *starting point* and go with them.

In fact, one of the unique features of this book is that it includes a chapter that supports you in doing just that. Chapter 11, "How to Invent Your Own Games," presents many helpful examples, guidelines, principles, and skills that you can use in adapting or creating your own cooperative games. We are confident that you will be able to go beyond the games described here, and thus fulfill our hope for the book—to encourage more "creative cooks," not just to offer a "cookbook."

Since learning to "cook" and adjust to a "noncompetitive diet" is a new experience for many people, we imagine that many readers will have questions as they get involved in this book and in the PLAYFAIR activities. In Chapter 12, "Questions and Answers About Play," we answer a baker's dozen commonly-asked questions about the implications and applications of cooperative approaches, how to get started, how to avoid pitfalls, and the impact that noncompetitive approaches can have.

After sorting through our answers and perspective on play, you might want to clarify some of your own thinking about this area. Drawing on several innovative

---

[12] For more information about PLAYFAIR see "Resources," Chapter 14.

Values Clarification activities, we invite you to take "A Value-able Look at Play" in Chapter 13.

Where do you go next? How can you extend your own thinking and uses of PLAYFAIR beyond the book? Chapter 14, "Resources," describes human, program, and written resources which you can use to springboard from this book into your own rich world of cooperative play.

# some tips on how to use this book

We've designed this book to contain "something for everybody." We don't expect that most readers are going to want to read it straight through cover to cover (although that's a perfectly fine way to do it!). Rather, we suspect that most people are going to jump around, reading the chapters and the games that are most relevant to their particular situations. If that is the case for you, we would recommend that you first read two chapters: Chapter Two, the one you've nearly finished right now (that was easy, wasn't it!), and Chapter Three, the section that immediately follows this one. That chapter is called "A Playful Sample: (How to Throw a Great Party)" and it's intended to give you an introduction to many of the different kinds of noncompetitive games, and to a

recommended way of sequencing and leading the games.

Using the sequence presented in Chapter 3 as a base, you can take a look at the different chapters and fill in other games for your specific group. For example, if you have a group of young people waiting for you on the playing field in half an hour you'll probably want to take a look at the "Energizers" chapter, and include a number of those in your play session. Or if you're getting together with a group of

people who don't know each other very well, then you'll probably want to plug in activities from the ''Mixer Games'' section.

If you're just about to throw a party, you might try out some of the games recommended for that purpose in the chapter called "Answers to Your Questions about Play." If it's a rainy Sunday afternoon and you're looking for something to do with your family, you'll want to pay careful attention to the ''Intimate and Family Games'' and the ''Mind Games'' chapters. The sequence presented in Chapter 3 can then be adapted to any number of specific play situations. You will find in Chapter 11 ''How to Invent your Own Games'' a list of helpful guidelines on how to pick games for your group.

Even though the games in this book have been divided into different categories, don't let that fool you—the divisions are just for convenience sake, and many of the games could easily fit into more than one category. Some of the ''Learning Games,'' for example, have been smash hits at many parties. And some of the ''Mind Games,'' although great for parties and family gatherings, have also made successful appearances in classrooms and business meetings.

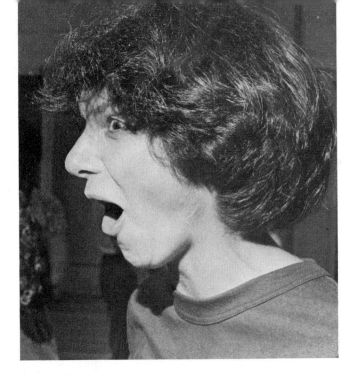

# a note on choosing partners and forming groups

A seemingly innocuous suggestion like ''Everybody pick a partner!'' can strike terror into the heart of many players. All sorts of questions race through people's heads:

- ''Should I pick somebody or wait to be picked?''

- ''What if nobody picks me?''

- ''What if I pick somebody and she doesn't want to play with me?''

- "How can I pick her without making her think I'm coming on to her?"

- "If I pick him, is he going to follow me around all day after this?"

- "Does he really want to play with me or is he just being polite?"

And on and on...

In order to create a safe and supportive play environment, it is important to invent ways to get the players into pairs and groups without anyone being left out, and without putting the players into anxiety-provoking positions. "Pick a partner" is interpreted by many people to mean "Get together with the person you are the most attracted to" and that is an embarrassing thing for many people to do openly. There are many random ways to get people into groups. The more specific you can be about your instructions, the more comfortable the players will be. We've suggested a number of these throughout the course of this book, for example:

- Put either your left thumb or your right pinky in the air, and get together with one other person who's doing the same thing you are.

- Put from zero to five fingers in the air and find one other partner so that when you add your fingers to that person's fingers you get an even number.

- Check to see whether you're wearing a belt or not. Find one other partner who, like you, is or is not wearing a belt.

- Find a partner who is wearing within two the same number of rings as you are.

- Start hopping around on either your right foot or your left foot and find a partner who is hopping with the same foot you are.

- Find a partner who has a different number of brothers and sisters than you do.

- Find a partner who is wearing one item of clothing the same color as you are.

There are lots of elements at play here: people looking carefully at each other, calling out things, moving around, raising their hands into the air—and you can decide which of those works best for your particular group and environment.

---

*I get very involved in games that have a blend of challenge and camaraderie.*

---

You could go on and on inventing these ways to get the players into pairs. In fact, that's a good idea! Get a group of people together and play THE PARTNER GAME. One person calls out a way to get people into partners, and everybody finds a partner through that method. Then somebody else calls out another way to get into partners, and everyone reshuffles into new pairs. There's no need to verbally criticize anybody's suggestions, since it will be evident as you move from one to the other which ones work and which don't.

In a few minutes your group can brainstorm dozens of usable pair-ups using this game. There are lots of interesting things you'll find out as the game goes on. For example, "Turn to your right and pick that person for your partner" sounds like a reasonable idea; however, as everybody turns to their right at once. . . "Put either your left hand or your right hand into the air, and pair up with someone who's doing the opposite" also sounds like a good suggestion. But suppose that only one person has her left hand in the air, and everyone else has their right hands in the air. You'll soon find out that if you give people two choices, they'll have to pair up with someone who has chosen *the same thing* as they have for it to work out in even pairs.

Forming the players into groups and teams is also something about which to be very careful. Many people have childhood memories of "choosing up teams," all the

while hoping not to be chosen last. Those feelings are still latent, even in the most confident of adults. Giving all the players a "forced-choice" and letting them select their teams simultaneously is an anxiety-free way of getting groups formed. For example, "Imagine that you could go on a vacation to the tropics as soon as you wanted to. If you'd rather go to Hawaii, go over there; if you want to go to Puerto Rico, over there; and if you want to go to Mozambique, over there." Voila: three groups! For most of the "team" games listed in this book it doesn't matter if the teams are of unequal size.

If you want to release somewhat more energy during the formation of the groups, you can let the groups sort themselves out without giving them specific meeting points. For example, "Decide if you would like to eat a banana, a peach, or a bunch of grapes right now. Get together in one large group with everyone else who wants to eat the same thing you do!"

Your choice of images from which players may choose should be tailored to the group with which you are working. Matt once did a PLAYFAIR for an overly excited group at a convention and he made the "mistake" of getting people into three teams as follows: "If you feel like being a walrus go to that side of the room; if you feel more like an elephant go to that side of the room; and if you feel more like a lion come over here." Pandemonium followed, with the walruses flapping their flippers

and barking loudly together, the elephants getting together in a big herd ready to attack the lions, and the lions roaring a challenge loud enough to totally drown out everyone else. Needless to say, the game was delayed while pandemonium "rained"!

# the playfair recipe

Before you move on to the sample play session coming up, we'd like to whet your appetite by offering you a checklist of ten playful ingredients for noncompetitive games. These ingredients for positive and nourishing play create a "recipe" for all of the games in this book. What's more, they can help you in concocting your own playful confections!

(1) Does the game have a good *sense of humor*? Does the game allow, or better yet, encourage the players to laugh with (as opposed to "laugh at") one another? Does the game reflect the notion that it makes sense to sometimes engage in non-sense?

(2) Is the game *cooperative* in nature? Can the participants play with, rather than play against, one another? Is the fun in the playing, and not in keeping score?

(3) Does the game take *positive action*? Are the players encouraged to support one another? Is there an absence of put-down statements? Do people feel better about themselves during and after playing the game?

(4) Is the game *inclusive* in nature? Are people encouraged to play, rather than to spectate? Are people accepted for who they are, as opposed to what they do? Do the players feel more connected with other people as a result of playing this game?

(5) Does the game provide opportunities for the players to be *imaginative and spontaneous*? Does the game provide room for re-creation—a chance for the players to change the rules?

(6) Do the players have *equality* in the game? Is this a game in which the "leader" is also one of the players?

(7) Can each player set his/her own *individual goals and standards*? Is there an absence of interpersonal judgmental statements? Can each player define her/his own pace? Does the game avoid putting players on-the-spot by having them "perform" in isolation and be "evaluated" in front of the group?

(8) Is the game *challenging*? Does the game have a sense of adventure to it? Can the players feel competent while playing this game?

(9) Does this game put *people before rules*? In other words, is the focus on the players rather than on the game? Do the players have a chance to celebrate themselves and their own playfulness?

(10) The last one is the simplest of all: is the game *fun*?

# 3 a playful sample: (how

Before constructing any play session, you will need some basic information about your group. You can ask yourself questions such as:

What ages are the players?

How mobile or physically active are the players?

How long will the session last?

What are the specific aims/goals of this session?

How well do the players know each other already? What is their history of playing together?

Obviously there can be many possible "sample play sessions," as many as there are situations in which it is possible to play noncompetitively with a group. So, in designing this sample, we have had to make some arbitrary decisions in an attempt to set up a model session that would cover as much ground as possible.

We've planned for an imaginary group of twenty physically mobile participants, ranging in age from sixteen to sixty. Some of the players are already friends, however most are strangers to each other. This will be a one-hour "introductory" play session for the players, and if it is successful it will be the beginning of a series of weekly playing-together sessions. Our goals for the session are to create a climate where the players can feel comfortable with each other, learn each other's names, and get a sense of what a "supportive play community" is all about.

In this sample play session we have tried to give you an idea of the range of possible games from which to choose. In the "Comments" section following each game you will find a listing of other games in this book that will go well with it.

# to throw a great party!)

The first thing we want to do is to give the players a chance to get to know each other a bit, so we'll begin the session with a physically active icebreaker called INCORPORATIONS, just one of the ''sampler'' games this chapter offers:

**incorporations**
**imaginary ball toss**
**moonwalk**
**the human spring**
**off balance**
**brussels sprouts**
**standing ovation**
**big wind blows**
**crescendo**
**wonderful circle**

# incorporations

Directions to the Players: **This is a game about forming and reforming groups as quickly as possible. I'm going to bang the cowbell (or blow the whistle, or turn on the siren, or flick the lights on and off, or whatever else you can think of to get the group's attention...Have some fun with this part!) and call out a group for you to get into. Don't worry if you're not even into the first group by the time I call out the second group, just head right for the second group. The idea is to meet as many people as you can in as many different groups as fast as possible. Okay (BONG!) Get into a group of three...(BONG!) Three plus one:...(BONG!) Get into a group of five so that everyone in your group has one item of clothing the same color as you do...(BONG!) Think of your phone number. Think of the last digit in your phone number. Get together with every single person here who is thinking of the same number you are...(BONG!) Get into a group of three people and make the letter H with your bodies...(BONG!) Find four other people born in the same season as you are...link pinkies in a circle with those four people, and jump up and down nine times with them...**

Comments: INCORPORATIONS is an excellent high-energy mixer for people who are first meeting each other. We've chosen INCORPORATIONS to start this session because it gives the players a chance to release — in a fast-paced, fun-filled way — some of their initial nervousness about being with a new group. INCORPORATIONS also gives the participants an easy introduction to the types of activities to come in the rest of the session: fast-moving physical interactions, physical contact with other people, quick verbal interactions, a bit of silliness, some creative thinking (''make the letter H with your bodies''), the feeling of ''instant'' community with the people in their small group formations.

The number of groupings and subgroupings the leader can think of for INCORPORATIONS is endless: you'll probably want to think of ones that are particularly appropriate for your players. There is no limit to the number of people who can play this game at once — the more people you are playing with, the more madcap energy the groupings can release!

INCORPORATIONS is a game where the play leader is totally in control, calling out the directions and putting the players through their paces. As the play session progresses, control of the games moves to the players and away from the leader. At first, however, it's fine if the leader takes most of the responsibility for making things happen.

INCORPORATIONS was invented by Bernie DeKoven.

If you like INCORPORATIONS, you'll probably also like BIRTHDAYS and CHORALE OF THE VOWELS in Chapter 4, two games that are spin-offs from INCORPORATIONS. If you want the players to learn each other's names, you can easily add that as part of the instructions for the forming of the groups. Since we think that having the players learn each other's names is an essential early component of forming a supportive play community, the next game in this sequence, IMAGINARY BALL TOSS, is designed to accomplish just that.

# imaginary ball toss

Directions to the Players: **Let's all stand together in a circle . . .**

**Take a look at the imaginary tennis ball that I have in my right hand. Notice that it has weight and size, and that although I can close my left hand into a fist right now, I can't close my right hand because the ball is in there. And when I throw it up in the air, like this, and catch it in the other hand, now I can't close my left hand.**

**I'm going to call out someone's name and throw the ball to that person. After catching it, she or he will call out someone else's name and throw the ball to that person. Don't worry if you don't know the name of someone you want to throw the ball to — just ask! Let's try to have everybody catch it once before anybody catches it a second time. And as we go around the circle, try to remember as many names as you can...Okay, what's your name?**

**FIRST PLAYER: Marty.**
**LEADER: Okay Marty, here it comes. (Throws ball)**
**MARTY: Mary. (Throws ball)**
**MARY: Jeanie. (Throws ball)**
**JEANIE: What's your name?**
**JERRY: Jerry.**
**LEADER: Jeanie, it's no longer a tennis ball, it's a basketball.**
**JEANIE: Jerry, catch! (Throws basketball)**

**LEADER: Jerry, it's no longer a basketball, it's a watermelon.**
**JERRY: Joanna. (Throws watermelon)**
**LEADER: Joanna, from now on, whoever catches it can either keep the object the same, or can change it to anything he or she wants to. So each time, we'll call out the name of the object we're throwing and then the name of the person we want to catch it.**
**JOANNA: It's a shot-put. Amaran.**
**AMARAN: It's still a shot-put. Ritch.**
**RITCH: It's an egg. Michael.**
**MICHAEL: It's a live chicken. Mahalia....**

**Comments:** IMAGINARY BALL TOSS is an excellent way for the players to get to know each others' names. It's also great fun, and a chance for the players to delight each other with the unusual objects they can think up to toss to each other. Oftentimes a crazy logic will evolve, with the objects flowing naturally into each other as they continually transform from one thing to the next.

Chapter 4, "Mixer Games" contains a number of other name games and get-acquainted games that could be used in conjunction with (or instead of) the first two games in this sample play session. For example, if you wanted to make *sure* that the players learned each others' names the first day you might want to follow IMAGINARY BALL TOSS with INTRODUCTIONS, especially if your group is a large one, and then follow that with the MOVING NAME GAME.

With the players starting to feel more comfortable with each other, it is time to move into some more energetic physical activities. We'll introduce them next to MOONWALK.

# moonwalk

Directions to the Players: **Join up with two other people. In this game, we're going to simulate what it might be like to take a jump where gravity is weaker than the earth's — like on the moon.**

**In each trio, one person stands in the middle, with hands on hips. The two partners stand on either side and grab the middle person's wrists and elbows, gently but firmly. The person in the middle counts down "Three...two...one!" and on "one!" jumps high into the air. At the same time the two partners lift the jumper gently into the air, giving some extra support to allow a jump which is higher than normal. Just give a bit of an extra lift — don't fling or heave or toss your jumper into the air!**

**When you're in the middle, keep your hands firmly planted on your hips the whole time. If you keep your hands on your hips, then your partners can really help control your flight, and can make sure you have a soft landing. Each of you will get a turn being the person in the middle. Make sure your threesome is far enough away from the other groups so that you won't crashland into anyone else. Decide who's going to take the first moonwalk, and blast off!**

**Comments:** MOONWALK is a good transition experience from the whole-group games with which this play session started to the two-person games that are coming up next. MOONWALK provides an exhilarating physical rush for the players, and often has them screaming and applauding. At the same time, it is an introduction to assisting and taking care of another person in a way that contributes to building a feeling of trust, support, and community.

You really can't get a feeling for this one by reading about it — get two friends and try it out! We learned about MOONWALK from Harry Schiller; he says that he learned it from somebody else, but he can't remember who it was.

Jeanie Cochran (one of the senior members of the PLAYFAIR staff) invented an even more energetic variation of MOONWALK that she calls MOONHOP. MOONHOP proceeds in much the same fashion as MOONWALK, except that each player takes five rapid hops in succession, moving forward all the time, while the hopper's two partners run alongside, lifting the hopper into the air with each great leap forward. The hopper pauses for barely a second between each successive hop, and the overall effect is almost like flying through the air.

If the physically active games like this one and the three that follow are working well with your group, you'll be interested in the other games like these in chapter 6.

Another game which is based on the notion of partners supporting one another is THE HUMAN SPRING. This is the next game we will play as we continue to build a sense of trust and community among the players.

# the human spring

Directions to the Players: **Are you wearing shoelaces? Get together with one other person, who, like you, is or is not wearing shoelaces...Stand about two feet away from each other, with your palms out facing your partner, at about chest level. Have your feet together. The idea of THE HUMAN SPRING is for you and your partner to lean forward simultaneously, let your hands meet in the middle and break your fall together, and then push off and spring backwards together, so you're back in your original position without losing your balance. It doesn't matter if one of you is bigger or heavier than the other — the idea is to get a rhythm and a balance going between you, to figure out the best way to do it over and over again with your particular bodies. So tune into your partner and adjust the strength of your spring to his or her particular needs...**

Now that you've got that mastered, you might try taking a step further back to increase the distance between you... Or try it with one hand...Or with arms crossed ... Or with legs crossed... Or on one leg ...Or with one person closing her eyes... Or whatever you can think of!

**Comments:** THE HUMAN SPRING was invented by Pamela Kekich and Bernie DeKoven in a park in Philadelphia one day, and it's a wonderful example of the way a competitive game can be transformed into a cooperative one. It is adapted from a game called ''Stand Off,'' which starts in the same basic position, but whose object is to knock your opponent off balance by slapping palm-to-palm against each other.

THE HUMAN SPRING is a good warm-up activity for a sequence of physically-active games (like the ones that follow in this play session). It's also a good game for leading into some of the partner games (like WRIST DANCING and FINGER DANCING) in the ''Intimate and Family Games'' chapter, and to the game which follows, OFF BALANCE. Like HUMAN SPRING, OFF BALANCE requires partners to work together so that both ''win.''

# off balance

Directions to the Players: **Find a partner who was born in a different month than you...Stand facing your partner, firmly grasping each other's hands or wrists, whichever feels more comfortable to the two of you. This game is called OFF BALANCE and its object is for both of you to be off balance, yet totally supporting each other the whole time. Now lean your weight backwards, so that if it weren't for your partner supporting you, you'd fall over...**

**Be careful not to put too much strain on your partner now — really try to work out an effective counterbalance between the two of you. Move around together, exploring different levels, different points of balance for your body. Use the support from your partner to explore things that you couldn't do by yourself — you might try leaning backwards balanced on one leg, pivoting around close to the ground — try all sorts of things. Be sure you support each other.**

**Now stand back-to-back with your partner, leaning into each other, so once again you're off balance and supporting each other's weight. Move around and explore this new position with the same idea you had when you were holding hands — you're both continually off balance yet continually supporting each other...**

**You and your partner join together with another pair now, to make up a group of four...The four of you try out a number of ways to be off balance together as a foursome. Again, start out carefully.**
**Comments:** OFF BALANCE can be an earth-shaking experience for the participants! If you don't build in the proper safety guidelines, they could have quite an unpleasant crash landing. The main thing for the facilitator to do is to keep the pace of the game quite moderate. If the interactions between the players start getting frenetic, slow them down before they get hurt. What often happens to players who are doing OFF BALANCE for the first time is that they occasionally overshoot their point of balance beyond their ability to control it, and both partners tumble to the ground. If the partners have been moving slowly and gently and are tuned-in to each other, they usually have a good shared laugh together. If they are careening wildly about the space together at high speed and then they fall, however...

One obvious word of caution to teachers: play this game with your students out-of-doors, in a gymnasium, or in any wide-open space. But *not in the classroom*! Any space where the players can stumble into desks or chairs (or even walls!) is taking too high a risk with their safety.

But let's not go overboard with the warnings. OFF BALANCE is not all that dangerous, and can be done quite safely. It's an extraordinary physical experience of paying attention to, being supported by, and non-verbally harmonizing with another person.

Incidentally, you'll notice that we almost never encourage the players to simply "choose" partners, but instead offer them a number of safe and nonthreatening alternatives. For a further rationale for this method, and suggestions about ways to divide groups and pick partners, see Chapter 2.

After OFF BALANCE we are ready to move from pairs and trios into a series of whole-group games. If you would like to continue with more partner games at this point, you will find some in the "Intimate And Family Games" chapter. The first of our large-group samplers is BRUSSELS SPROUTS.

# brussels sprouts

Directions to the Players: **BRUSSELS SPROUTS is a tag game that starts out in slow motion. If I'm "It," and I'm chasing Susan in slow motion and I catch her, instead of the It passing from me to her, we link up arms and we are It together. And the next person we capture also links up arms with us. The It gets larger and larger until it encompasses everyone, and that's the end of the game.**

**Now, at any time any of the players can call out "Lima Beans!". That changes the speed of the game from slow motion to fast** motion, or from fast motion back to slow motion. At any time anyone can also call out "Brussels Sprouts!". That has no effect on the game whatsoever.

**Any of the people who are linked together to form the It can call out at any time the word "Carrots!". This means that the people in the It unlink arms, jump up in the air, spin around, and link up again facing in the opposite direction.**

**Remember that we start in slow motion. Who wants to be the beginning of the It?**

**Comments:** The genesis of this game is discussed in some detail in Chapter 11, "How To Invent Your Own Games." With more than thirty players BRUSSELS SPROUTS can get a bit out of hand, so we recommend its close cousin, AMOEBA TAG (Chapter 6) for use with large groups. The beauty of BRUSSELS SPROUTS is that It always wins — It just gets bigger and bigger until everyone is linked together on the same team!

Here's some additional food-for-thought: the word "it" has many negative connotations. In competitive tag games, the first thing the players call out is "not it." "It" is seen as undesirable, and something to be avoided at all costs. In order to help players see the "it" as another human being (and not as an object or dreaded disease), we often encourage players to use "center person" in place of "it." It's quite a simple word change, but we've seen this change bring about significant positive changes in how people interact with their playmates.

Allowing the players to change the speed of the game at will begins the process of giving the participants more and more control over the games in progress. In this sample play session, that process will reach its culmination in BIG WIND BLOWS, a game in which the players have total control over the game once it begins, including determining when the game is over and when to go on to the next game.

First, let's capitalize on the "team spirit" generated during BRUSSELS SPROUTS, and make our next stop a game in which we can applaud our "teammates," STANDING OVATION.

# standing ovation

Directions to the Players: **Have a seat, right where you are.**

Everybody gets depressed once in a while — that's just one of the facts of life. Some people feel there isn't much you can do about it, you've just got to take your lumps. But what we're trying to do here today is to create a special kind of supportive environment for each other, to create a place where we can each get a little bit of extra support, a little bit of extra nourishment for ourselves. Maybe *you've* been having a tough time of it lately, maybe you've had a tough day today, or a tough week, or a tough month. I'm not going to ask you to explain to us what's been going on for you. But if you've been having a tough time of it lately, what I am going to do is give you a very special opportunity to get a bit of support and nourishment and celebration for yourself.

If for any reason you have been having something of a hard time of it lately and you feel like you could use some support for yourself right now, would you come stand up here right next to me . . . (several people go to the front) . . . Let's hold hands, facing everybody else . . .

Okay, you see before you a group of people who for one reason or another have been having something of a tough time of it lately — let's give these people the most incredibly spectacular, thunderous standing ovation they've ever seen!!! . . .

Let's make an agreement . . . At any time during the remainder of this play session anybody can get to their feet and say "I want a standing ovation!" and no matter what we're doing we'll stop and give it to him or her. There's only one rule about that: you can't be real wimpy about it. If you're going to ask for one, then take it like you deserve it — jump up on a chair or jump up on this platform or get two people to hoist you up on their shoulders, and hold your hands over your head in a gesture of victory — go for it in a big way!

**Comments:** Why should performing artists be the only ones who get to savor a standing ovation? We all deserve it! A standing ovation should be reserved not only for a special occasion, but for a special person as well. And that means all of us! It feels wonderful to receive, and it can be incredibly energizing to give one, too. It's a very warm, connected feeling to be a part of a group that is delivering a standing ovation, applauding what is human and wonderful about each other.

The larger the group, the more intense is the effect of a standing ovation. Of course it happens on occasion that the play leader paints such an attractive portrait of group support that everyone rushes up to receive some, leaving no one in the audience to give the standing ovation! Jerry Ewen (who heads PLAYFAIR'S West Coast division) once included STANDING OVATION at a university in Ohio. So many people responded to his invitation to come up on stage to receive some group support that the entire stage sank slowly to the ground under their combined weight!

The agreement that standing ovations can occur at any time during a play session adds a lovely dimension of tension and expectation to choosing the right moment to ask for an ovation for yourself. Players begin to take into account not only the time when it will do them the most good to receive one, but also the time when it will do the *group* the most good to give one. We often tell the players "If you have to leave the session early for some reason, don't just slink away — tell us that you have to go, share with us what you enjoyed about being with all of us, and ask us to send you off with a giant standing ovation!"

On many college campuses the concept of the standing ovation is one thing that lingers on long after the PLAYFAIR event itself is over. We often hear reports of students jumping up on a table in the cafeteria and bellowing out "I just finished

my Physics midterm and I want a standing ovation!", followed by a thunderous explosion of whistling, cheering, and table pounding by the assembled student body.

Building on the spirit and energy of STANDING OVATION, we continue with another game involving the whole group playing together, BIG WIND BLOWS.

# big wind blows

Directions to the Players: **BIG WIND BLOWS** is a game that we are going to play with a parachute.[1] ... Let's all form a circle around the parachute, with everyone holding on. The first thing to learn is the chant that goes with the game, ''What does the big wind blow?!'' So let's all try that together ... (''What does the big wind blow?'')

Anyone who is holding on to the parachute can call out any three numbers, like ''one ... eighteen ... ninety-four!'' and then we all lift the parachute up over our heads while chanting ''What does the big wind blow?'' Then, when the parachute hits its highest point, the person who called out the three numbers calls out a category that people might fall into — such as ''everybody wearing sneakers!'' If you are wearing sneakers, then you would run underneath the parachute and trade places on the other side with someone else who was also running underneath the parachute. If you don't fall into that category, then you keep holding the parachute up for the people who are running underneath it. Remember that the idea is *not* to try to trap people underneath the parachute.

Let's try one round of it, and one quick word of caution first — don't run full tilt under the parachute — run carefully because you can't see all that well under

there, and everybody is running towards the center, so you really could get into a collision if you're not careful ... Okay, let's go! Twenty ... twenty-one ... forty! (''What does the big wind blow?'') Everybody who had breakfast this morning! ...

Another thing to be very careful about is what kinds of categories you call out. This is one of those times where a lot of your competitive conditioning is going to come up and you may want to call out things to humiliate the other players. Try to avoid ''Everybody who is twenty pounds overweight!'' or ''Everybody with pimples!'' Don't put yourself down for it, because it's the way most of us have been taught to play. Just think about what you're going to say before you say it and make sure it's not putting anybody down or making anybody feel bad. Let's use categories that will help move us toward the sense of support and community that we're trying to create here!

A final question — when is this game over? Let's say that if somebody calls out a category and nobody runs, then the game is over for everybody. So that might happen accidentally — you might call out ''Everybody who had breakfast this morning!'' and it turns out that nobody had breakfast. Or you might decide to end the game on purpose by calling out something like ''Everybody born on the planet Pluto!''

**Comments:** We were a bit embarrassed at first by how ''preachy'' these instructions may sound. But it proved necessary to do it that way. We love this game, but we were ready to give it up because everytime we played it people would call out things that were offensive put-downs (e.g. ''everybody who thinks they are ugly,'' ''all the cute chicks''). As a first defense, we tried giving the instructions but not participating in the actual playing of the game — but that made no sense, because it isolated us from the rest of the play community. And once in a while we would overhear something that would drive us crazy, anyway. Finally, we realized that we could be more up-front about our expectations before the game began — and it changed the tenor of the game completely for us. Now when we play BIG WIND BLOWS it's fun for everybody — *including us.*

The final question posed in the Directions to the Players — ''When is this game over?'' — is a very interesting one for the play leader. There are many different ways to end a game, and in a game like this one in which we are trying to give the players more and more control over the game, it makes sense to give them control over the end of the game as well. For a further discussion on ways to end a game, see the Comments following TOUCH BLUE, (Chapter 9).

After a series of physically active games like these, it's time to give the players a bit of a rest. So we follow BIG WIND BLOWS with CRESCENDO, a less physically demanding (although by no means less energetic!) activity.

[1]Don't have a parachute? See Chapter 11!

# crescendo

Directions to the Players: **Pick a partner on the opposite side of the group from you, whose name you didn't know before you came here today. Get together . . .**

   **We're going to play a sound-and-movement game called CRESCENDO, and my partner (Eric) and I are going to demonstrate it first, then you and your partner are going to get to play it together. We're going to stand facing each other, a couple of feet apart, and tune into each other's breathing. I'm going to start the game by showing Eric a sound-and-a-motion that he can easily repeat. It doesn't have to make literal sense, however. So I might jump up and down and scream, like this . . . Or I might reach out gently towards Eric's cheek and say seductively, "Oooohhh." Notice that I start very softly with my sound and with a very small movement, and as the game continues I'm going to get louder and bigger, building to a crescendo pitch, and then coming down gradually to soft and small again.**

   **Eric is going to exactly mimic what I'm doing, both in my gestures and my voice, at the same time that I'm doing it. So when I get louder and bigger, he also gets louder and bigger, and as I get softer and smaller, he also gets smaller and softer. So he'll try to follow my lead exactly, and then after we've come back down to small and soft,**

**we'll switch roles and he'll become the leader while I become the follower. Let's try that much right now. Ready, Eric? . . .**

   **Would you and your partner right now take a moment to decide which one of you is going to be lemonade and which one is going to be grapefruit juice? . . . I'd like the people who picked grapefruit juice to be the leaders the first time around. Okay, would you stand facing each other, and tune into each other's breathing? Grapefruits remember to start softly and build up gradually to a crescendo, and then back down to soft again . . . Then we'll switch the lead to the lemons . . .**

**Comments:** CRESCENDO requires the two partners to sensitively tune-in to each other, and in that respect it builds upon the skills and sharing that have been introduced in the rest of the play session. It is much easier for the players to have a successful experience of CRESCENDO after they have first played IMAGINARY BALL TOSS, THE HUMAN SPRING, and OFF BALANCE.

CRESCENDO can be used as the middle game in a three game sequence, with HOW TO START AN ARGUMENT, and REBOUND. A number of teachers have used this sequence to focus on verbal and non-verbal communication, and the three games flow into each other quite naturally. Each one is higher risk than the one that preceeded it, and each one builds on the safety and skills of the one preceeding and pushes the players to extend themselves more.

If the group with whom you are playing is somewhat self-conscious, we would advise you to substitute ARGUMENT in place of CRESCENDO here. Because CRESCENDO uses ''sounds'' rather than ''words'' it can be a more threatening game for some players than ARGUMENT, which is similar in style but which uses actual ''words.''

We like to end every play session by giving the players a chance to share their appreciations for each other, so with that in mind we'll conclude this session with a game called WONDERFUL CIRCLE. (Incidentally, STANDING OVATION is a delightfully enthusiastic way to share appreciation, and this would be a good time for that too, if you haven't already!)

# wonderful circle

Directions to the Players: **When was the last time your best friend told you how wonderful he or she thinks you are? When was the last time the people at work told you what a joy it is to see you every day?**

The older we get, the less we get to hear from other people about what we're doing well. So let's take some time right now to share with each other what it is that we've liked about playing together today. And you know that we've all been trained very well to do the opposite of that — everyone here is probably an expert at saying what it is we *don't* like about something. Being "critical" is something we've all been praised for in the past, so we've all become good at it. I want you to put that critical side of you aside right now, and concentrate on *appreciating* your experience here today. We've tried to create a safe, supportive place here, where people can feel a sense of community, and experiment with learning about cooperation with each other. Critical judgments don't serve any constructive purpose toward that goal.

Let's get into a big circle with our arms around each other's waists . . . Find out the names of the people you're holding on to on either side of you . . . We'll start taking baby steps to the left, and we'll keep going to the left until somebody says "Stop!" Then that person will share something she or he felt good about playing with the other people here today. You might want to say something you felt good about yourself: something you discovered about your own playfulness. Or you might want to appreciate a positive interaction you had with one other player. Or you might want to share good feelings you had about the group as a whole, and what being in a supportive environment like we created today meant to you. The only guideline I'd like to offer is that you don't talk about the *games* you played, but about the *people* you played them with.

When you've finished your brief sharing, say "Go!", and we'll all take baby steps in the other direction until someone else says "Stop!" and shares something she or he is feeling good about. When you have a sense that everyone who wants to take a turn has taken a turn — and not everyone has to go, of course — then you say "Stop!" and you ask "Are we done yet?" If someone in the circle still has something more to share with the group, then that person says "No — Go!", and we continue moving around in our circle, and someone else can ask the question again later. If the question is followed by ten seconds of silence, we know that the game is over and we'll all rush into the center of the circle and give ourselves a gigantic standing ovation!

**Comments:** One of the very special things about the WONDERFUL CIRCLE (which was invented by Pamela Kekich) is that it combines playful, physical movement with the sharing of some very personal information. We are great believers in the proposition that a group's attention span will be much greater if there is physical activity interspersed with talking and listening, and the WONDERFUL CIRCLE does this very well.

A WONDERFUL CIRCLE can be an emotionally moving and uplifting experience, with dozens (or hundreds!) of people holding onto each other, beaming at each other, and sharing words of support and appreciation and mutual good-feeling.

WONDERFUL CIRCLE could also be easily adapted for use in ongoing task groups as well as play groups. What a wonderful way to end the day at school, or at the office. Or what a powerful beginning it might be to a staff meeting or a family dinner to have the participants appreciate *each other* before they begin their devouring!

You'll find some alternative ways to end a play session described in the "Endings" chapter.

The sequence of ten games presented in this chapter will give you a playful taste of the different "flavors" of cooperative games you can use in your own setting. We hope they have whetted your appetite for the chapters to come, which introduce additional games that can be used with a variety of groups and for a variety of purposes!

# 4 mixer games: breaking the

"What do other people here think of me?"

"Will I fit in?"

"I'm afraid I might make a fool of myself in front of these new people."

"Will anybody approach me . . . or should I make the first move in meeting others?"

"I'm afraid they'll reject me, put me down, or laugh at me if I take the initiative."

Do any of these thoughts or feelings sound familiar? Chances are that you — like we — have experienced these at one time or another when you were new to a group (and/or when the group itself was "new"). Every day, people join groups or form groups. Inevitably, these kinds of questions come up: *identity* ("Who am I in relation to this group? How do I see myself, and how do others see me?); *connectedness* ("Do I belong here? Will I be accepted? Who are my friends or allies in this group?"); and *power* ("Can I make a difference in this group? Will other people listen to me and

# ice

my ideas? How can I feel like an important, influential member of the group? Will I be able to contribute to the group? Will people notice me and my contributions?''). As long as people are pre-occupied with these kinds of questions, concerns, and fears, they will not function well as a group. This is true whether the group is a classroom (if students' minds are on these questions, they will have little attention for learning), an office or meeting (people focusing on how to ''protect themselves'' have less to give to the task at hand, and are less productive), or a new group of students at college (who may be so intent on ''being cool'' that they are frozen in their tracks when it comes to reaching out and meeting new people).

Ice-breakers or mixers can be excellent devices to help people feel more comfortable with themselves and with others and feel more ''at home'' in the group. They free attention from the pre-occupying questions and permit focus on the task at hand — learning (in a school setting), productivity (in a business setting), meeting people (in a freshman orientation). The mixer games are short and sweet and effective in helping people ''get it together.''

---

*I am most playful when I am not under pressure or tension. Games that are effective ice-breakers or warm-up activities for me are ones that bring my attention out by reducing the tension I feel. I realized that detached concentration is the key to being playful for me — when I can detach myself from ''reality'' and concentrate on creating a new, playful, cooperative ''reality''.*

---

There are two basic flavors of mixers: connectors and name games. Connectors encourage people to break the larger group into smaller groups as a way of helping people to ''make a connection'' with

another person(s). For instance, you'll find INTRODUCTIONS, BIRTHDAYS, ANIMALS, HUM-DINGER, CHORALE OF THE VOWELS, and the HUMAN TREASURE HUNT in this chapter. All are activities which "break up cliques," invite people to form random groupings, and give people permission to meet others in a non-threatening and fun way. Name games are good for helping participants get to know one another. When people feel recognized (by name) and when they can recognize others, they are well on the way to feeling "at home" in their group. Some creative ways to help people learn others' names can be found in several games in this chapter — INTRODUCTIONS, MOVING NAME GAME, SINGING NAME GAME, and HUMAN TREASURE HUNT.

You'll notice several things about these games. First, some (INTRODUCTIONS, HUMAN TREASURE HUNT) are a mixture of the two flavors above — they serve *both* as connectors and as ways to learn names. Second, there are a number of variations in the two flavors — some games involve physical movement (MOVING NAME GAME, HUM-DINGER), some involve singing (SINGING NAME GAME, CHORALE OF THE VOWELS), some involve people in contacting others one at a time (HUMAN TREASURE HUNT, INTRODUCTIONS), some require people to work with a group (BIRTHDAYS, CHORALE OF THE VOWELS).

We encourage you to mix the flavors and variations to fit the particular needs of your group, classroom, or family. Mixers can be used to set the tone for your time together, can encourage people to feel "safe", and can evoke lots of laughter in releasing tension.

**introductions**
**moving name game**
**singing name game**
**birthdays**
**animals**
**hum-dinger**
**chorale of the vowels**
**human treasure hunt**

# introductions

Directions to the Players: **Imagine this is your birthday and you have called all of us together for a giant birthday party. You know everybody here, but nobody else knows anybody at all. So of course you want to get us all to meet each other. So your job in the next three minutes is to introduce everybody here to everybody else here. Don't introduce yourself to anybody, just go up to someone like this and say "Hi, what's your name?" ("Paula.") "Hi Paula, come on, I'd like you to meet somebody ... Hi, what's your name?" ("Dave.") "Hiya Dave, this is Paula, Paula this is Dave." Now, when you get introduced to somebody, really do it up right — get a good look at the person, shake hands, give a big smile ... Okay, do you have the idea? You have three minutes to introduce everybody here to everybody else! Go to it!**

**Comments:** In the frenzy of activity that INTRODUCTIONS creates, it actually is impossible to really remember a lot of people's names. But you will learn some, and you'll get introduced to many people who will be excited about meeting you. The best thing about this game is that it creates an overriding spirit of friendliness and taking care of each other. In one big burst of enthusiastic energy it enables the participants to get rid of a lot of the tension we all experience when first getting together with a new group.

We're aware of numerous classrooms in which the students don't even know the names of the people sitting next to them. If you are interested in developing a "learning community" in your classroom, a good first step might be to have the students learn each other's names in a light-spirited way such as INTRODUCTIONS.

# moving name game

Directions to the Players: **Let's get into one big circle . . . Think of the name that you like to be called, and think of how many beats or syllables are in that name. For instance, if I wanted to be called ''Pamela'' there would be three beats; if I wanted to be called ''Pam'' there would be just one beat . . .**

**Okay, got that? Take a minute to move around in your space and come up with a series of movements so that there is one distinct and easily repeatable movement for each beat in your name. It doesn't have to be anything elaborate — a movement of your arm is perfectly okay . . .**

**We'll start with me, and I'll say my name and do my three movements at the same time. And then we'll all say the name and do my three movements. Let's try that. Pam-e-la. (''PAM-E-LA''). Great. Now the person on my left will go, and he'll show us his name-and-movement, and then we'll all do his name-and-movement together, and then we'll all do my name-and-movement and his name-and-movement. Then we'll go on to the person on his left, and she'll show us her name-and-movement. Then we'll all do her name-and-movement. And then we'll do my name-and-movement, and the second person's name-and-movement, and the third person's name-and-movement, all in rapid succession! Then we'll go on to the fourth person and do the same**

thing, until we've gone all the way around the circle.

**Make sure that you look at each person whose name-and-movement you're doing each time, and that will help you to remember his or her name.**

**Comments:** This can be an effective and enjoyable way to get to know people's names — coupling the movement with the name seems to help people's memories. In fact, some PLAYFAIR participants who met each other months after having played this name game could remember each other's movements, as well as their names! If your name circle has more than 10 players in it, you might want to break it up after ten people and start the sequence over again, so the game won't take all day. After you've gone all the way around once, it's sometimes fun to have the players go through each other's names and movements in the reverse order from the one in which they learned them. Or do the movements in sequence without the names. Or skip around randomly. Or lots of other variations you can think of.

This name game is generally done as an introductory activity for a group, near the beginning of a play session or the beginning of the group's life. However, several elementary school teachers have reported to us that they've done it over and over again during the course of the school year with the same students making up different movements each time, and that it's always a big hit.

We have also done this activity with a group of people who know each other quite well (an office staff, employees at a business or hospital, a staff development training session at a university). When the people already know each other's names, we have asked them to take pseudonyms for the duration of the play session: ''Pick the name that you've always wanted to be called if you had the choice!''

People who see each other every day in a work environment often develop fairly rigid, hierarchical relationships with each other, and those day-to-day relationships inhibit their ability to let go and be playful with each other. This game can be used with groups that work together, and can be helpful in cutting through those everyday relationships, so that the co-workers can begin to relate to each other in a new, more fun-filled and more supportive way. Taking pseudonyms is an easy way to let the participants announce some of their playful fantasies about their lives (''My name is Marshmallow.''), and to begin re-meeting each other afresh.

The first three games in this chapter are our variations of games originally developed by Bernie DeKoven (INTRODUCTIONS) and Pamela Kekich (MOVING NAME GAME and SINGING NAME GAME). For further information on these two playful people, see the ''Resources'' chapter.

# singing name game

Directions to the Players: **Let's get into one big circle ... On the count of three, I'd like you to sing out your first name as loudly as you can ... Ready? One ... two ... three!!! ...**

**Now take a moment and develop a little movement sequence that you can do in the same time that it takes you to sing out your name. It can be one big continuous movement, or a quick series of smaller movements. You can be jumping up in the air, or just moving your eyeballs around in circles — any kind of movement is fine! Whatever you want to do. Take a minute to practice getting your name and your movement synchronized together ...**

**We're going to go around the circle very rapidly, doing our names-and-movements one after the other, moving to the right. I'm going to start, and then the person on my right is going to do hers the instant I'm finished. Even if she starts before I'm quite finished, that's okay, we don't want any silent space at all! And then when she's just about finished, the person on her right is going to let 'er rip. As fast as we can go. Okay, is everybody all set? ... Mike! ... Muriel! ... Woody! ...**

Comments: If you are playing with a very large group, you'll probably want to have several circles going at once, instead of one gigantic one (although that has been done!).

It's important to keep the pace of this activity very fast, or else it becomes a "performance" of various "routines", and the whole light-hearted spirit of the thing can be lost.

If you are playing with participants who are shy with each other at first, and who might be hesitant to do the singing or the movement part of this game, then save this activity until after you have done some of the games from the "Energizers" chapter with your group. After a few of those games, most groups develop a spirit of "What's next — we're ready for anything!" If your group is shy about singing, you may wish to precede this game with HUM-DINGER.

There are lots of possible variations on the basic SINGING NAME GAME. One simple one that we like is to get the players into pairs (see Chapter 2 for a discussion of some non-threatening ways to help the players get into pairs) and to have them teach their singing name-and-motion to each other. From there the partners can share their newly-learned name-and-motion back in the circle formation, or simultaneously all-at-once, or alternating back and forth several times between the partners — or whatever else you can think of!

# birthdays

Directions to the Players: **When I blow this whistle, I'd like you to get together as quickly as possible with everybody here who was born in the same month as you were. (TWEET!) . . . . Get together in a tight group with the people from your month, away from the other months. I'm going to call out the names of the months, and when I call out your month, give me a big cheer. And if you see two groups cheering for the same month — if there are two small groups of Januaries, for example — then get yourselves together into one big January. Okay, January! . . . February! . . . March! . . . .**

**When you hear the whistle you're going to have one minute in your group to develop and rehearse a group cheer for your month, so (TWEET!) go to it, Cheerleaders! . . . .**

**Sit down with your month, and we're going to show our cheers like this: first January will spring to its feet and do its cheer. As soon as January sits down, February will leap to its feet and do its cheer, and we'll go right through the year, one month after the other, bam! bam! bam!, and as soon as December is finished and sits down we'll all rise to our feet and give ourselves a standing ovation.**

Comments: Players often feel a strong sense of "identification" and "belonging" to the other people born in their month. This group-within-the-group is a place of safety and high spirits. However, these high spirits can easily spill over into becoming competitive, with each group "performing" and trying to be "the best." Keeping the pace of the game very rapid (unlike the pace of a "contest" where each entry is carefully judged), and saving all the applause until the standing group ovation at the end, are both effective ways to diffuse the competitive possibilities of BIRTHDAYS.

If you are playing with a small group, you can achieve the same effect by having the players divide up according to the *season* in which they were born, rather than the month.

# animals

Directions to the Players: **Would someone give me the name of an animal that makes a sound we can all repeat easily? ("A cow.") A cow. And what kind of sound does that make? ("Moo".) Okay, let's all try that together. (MOO!!) Great. Who has another one? ("A dog.") A dog. How does that go? ("Rarrf! Rarrf!") Let's all try that one. (RAARF!! RARRF!!) And now the cow. (MOO!!) Who has a third one — an animal and the sound it makes. ("A wolf.") A wolf — and show us what that sounds like. ("Aooooo ...") Let's everybody try the wolf on three. One ... two ... three ... (AOOOOO!! ...) And now the dog. (RARRF!!) And the cow. (MOOOO!!)**

**Close your eyes now, and picture those three animals standing side by side, the dog, the cow, and the wolf. All of a sudden there is a loud noise and two of them run away. Take a good look at the one animal that is remaining in your mind. Open your eyes and make the noise of that one remaining animal, and get together in a group here with everyone else who is making the same noise you are.**

**Comments:** One variation of this game is to play all the way through with everyone's eyes closed. However, you should be aware that this can make the game much more threatening to some people. So, think carefully about your group before you decide which variation to play. Either way, there is bound to be a lot of noise and a lot of laughter!

"Rehearsing" the animal noises with the large group first seems to make it much less embarrassing for the players to walk around making the noises on their own — it's a way of giving them "permission" to play.

# hum-dinger

Directions to the Players: **How many of you can sing? . . . . Okay, now what happened to you when I asked that very simple question? What were you thinking, what did you feel, and what did you observe yourself doing (or not doing) behaviorally? Let's hear a couple of your responses . . . (Oh, no!'' . . . ''PLEASE, don't ask me to sing in front of the group!'')**

**Now, you'll notice that I did not ask ''how many of you can sing well?'' and I didn't say ''how many of you would like to do a solo in front of the group?'' It's incredible that so many of us have internalized ''vultures'' that tell us we can't sing. Is it any wonder, when so many of us have had an adult tell us at one point or another to ''mouth'' the words (because we're ''throwing everyone else off.'')?**

**This game, I hope, will help us all to dump the vulture that tells us we can't sing. This is going to be a hum-dinger of a game! What we need to do first is make a list on the board of some songs that everyone would know — I'll record them as you suggest them . . . For instance, ''Row, Row, Row Your Boat'' would be one that all of us are familiar with. Who has another? . . . . (''Star Spangled Banner'') (''Old MacDonald Had a Farm'') (''Happy Birthday'') (''Twinkle, Twinkle Little Star'') (''Jingle Bells'').**

**The next step is for each of you to literally take some steps. File by me, one-by-one — as you do, I'll whisper a sweet something in your ear — I'd like you not to tell anyone else what that secret is. Okay, come on up! (As each person files by, the play leader whispers in his/her ear one of the songs from the list) . . .**

**Now that you all have your secret words firmly between your ears, I'd like to present the following challenge to you: as quickly as possible, I'd like us each to find our hum-dinger partners. Now, how do we do that? The way we do it is by milling around the room, with each person humming the song I whispered in your ear. Find all the other people in this group who are humming the same song as you. Once you find one person, link up your arms, and keep going and see if you can keep growing by finding other people who are humming the same tune.**

**. . . . On your mark, get set, hum! . . .**

**Comments:** This is an excellent way to help people become un-self-conscious about singing. It can also make for quite a hilarious scene, as the players simultaneously hum and search for their co-hummers.

When working with a very large group, it would make more sense for each individual player to select from the list the song he/she will go around humming, rather than having the leader whisper it to each person.

After everybody has found their humdinger partners, you may want to engage in a humming medley by moving from group to group. In one such group medley, a woman who said she had not sung in forty years (she didn't raise her hand to the question ''how many of you can sing?'') spontaneously broke into singing (rather than humming) her song. She was surprised and pleased, and the group was delighted that she had re-discovered a long-lost part of herself!

# chorale of the vowels

Directions to the Players: **On the count of "Venus" I'd like you to call out your name as loudly as you can. Mars . . . Pluto . . . Venus!! . . . Now close your eyes for a few moments and think of the first vowel in your first name. In your mind I'd like you to imagine the most beautiful voice in the world singing that vowel. Listen to that beautiful voice for awhile . . . Now, I'd like you to reproduce it as nearly as you can. Begin singing out that beautiful vowel as strongly as you can . . . (A.E.I.O.U.Y.) . . . Okay, open your eyes and keep singing, and get together in as big a group as possible with everybody else who's singing your vowel . . . .**

   **Get into a tight group with the people with your vowel, and move your group into a space separate from all the other vowels . . . We are now almost ready for that incredible vocal masterwork, the** CHORALE OF THE VOWELS. **Who would like to conduct this masterpiece? . . . Okay, come on up where everybody can see you, grab your baton and see what you can create . . . Experiment with blending the vowels together and with letting them sing separately, with short notes and long notes, with soft ones and loud ones, and anything else you want to do with us . . . .**

Comments: Conducting a chorus like this can be a great joy, and it's something not many of us ever get to experience. Even people who think of themselves as "non-singers" are amazed at how beautiful their voice sounds when it's mixed in with a large group all singing the same vowel. Move over, Hallelujah Chorus — here comes the CHORALE OF THE VOWELS!!!!

# human treasure hunt

Directions to the Players: **How many of you have ever gone on a scavenger hunt? This kind of search-and-find mission usually involves people in looking for such obscurities as 3 matchbook covers, 2 pieces of broken glass, 5 round rocks, 1 apple core, etc.**

**We're about to engage in a hunt. But this kind of hunt will be different, 'cause what we'll be looking for can be found right in this group. In fact, what we'll be doing is taking off on a human treasure hunt, discovering the resources and treasures of the people in our group!**

**The purpose of this activity is for you to catch up on what has been happening in the lives of those people you already know and to get acquainted with people you don't know. Fill out as many as you can of the items on the sheet which I hand to each of you. Speak to the people — please do not use prior knowledge that you have about someone. Put the appropriate name in the space provided. Try to fill in one item for each person you contact ...**

**Are you ready to dig in? ... Begin! ...**

**Comments:** The HUMAN TREASURE HUNT is a fun-filled way to help the people in your group to meet each other and to learn a few things about each other. We've included a number of sample treasure hunt ''maps'' to give you a sense of the variety of possibilities in this game. By adapting the questions, this activity could be great fun for *any* age-level. You'll also notice that treasure hunts can be focused on particular themes — for instance, collecting the wisdom and experience people have about such issues as sexism, parenting, politics. Cook up a baker's dozen of your own — or better yet, have the players themselves lend helping hands/minds!

Many teachers use the HUMAN TREASURE HUNT as a diagnostic tool to identify the experiences, interests, and knowledge which students bring to the classroom. Other teachers employ it as a stimulus for team-building. Students who have similar interests (or students who would like to learn more about what another student already knows) can easily form work (or play) groups around that particular area. With different questions, the HUMAN TREASURE HUNT can be re-discovered on a regular basis — some groups like to start their meetings with a mini-version of the hunt every week!

Thanks to Lois Hart for sharing this activity with us.

# human treasure hunt #1: a baker's dozen (joel goodman)

1. Find 4 people who wonder what they ''want to be'' when they grow up.
2. Find 3 people who see themselves more as a ''funnybone'' than as a ''backbone''.
3. Find 5 people who have ways of showing caring in their own families that you like.
4. Find 2 people who feel that they have a good balance between their ''work life'' and their ''home life.'' Find out how they maintain their balance.
5. Find someone who feels that ''you can't fight city hall.''
6. Find 3 people who feel the same kind of stress on the job as you do. Ask some clarifying questions of one another.
7. Find 4 people who are religious readers of the PEANUTS comic strip.
8. Find 3 people who work at least ten hours each day. Find out what they enjoy the most about their jobs.
9. Find 4 people who have had a good laugh in the past week. What brought on the laughter?
10. Find someone who has ''bombed'' once in working with a group. Sit him/her on your lap while listening to the story.
11. Find 5 people who have heard at least three ''put-downs'' today.
12. Find 3 people who have gotten into a ''yelling argument'' with their child(ren)/parents at some point in the past. Have them whisper in your ear what it was about.
13. Find 2 people who see themselves as creative. Discover the key to their creativity.

# human treasure hunt #2: a baker's dozen (joel goodman, matt weinstein)*

1. Find someone who wears some item of clothing the same size as you do. Switch clothes with them!
2. Find someone who would like to have an uplifting experience this week. Give it to 'em!
3. Find someone who can sing three TV commercials. Lend 'em an ear.
4. Find someone whom you don't know. Do something about that.
5. Find someone who has a special place. Find out what makes it special.
6. Find someone who has something for lunch that you would like a bite of . . . bite on!
7. Find someone who needs a shot in the arm. Give it to 'em (figuratively).
8. Find someone who remembers a favorite game from age seven. Learn it!
9. Find someone who tends to get carried away in groups. Carry 'em away.
10. Find someone who can spit watermelon seeds as far as you can.
11. Find someone who is presently wrestling with a values dilemma in his/her own life. Lend a listening ear.
12. Find someone who has the same size thumb as you do.
13. Find someone who wouldn't mind getting a backrub from a total stranger. Rub a dub dub . . .

_____

·with help from Howard Kirschenbaum

# human treasure hunt #3: men, women, and sexism (margie ingram)

1. Find two people who had the same heroine/hero when they were growing up as you had.
2. Find two people who had a male elementary teacher when they were in school.
3. Find three people who believe it's o.k. for a man to cry.
4. Find two people who like being female/male for the same reason you like being male/female.
5. Find two people who had, when growing up, at least one close, purely "platonic" relationship with a person of the opposite sex.
6. Find three people who are totally happy they are either female/male.
7. Find three people who wish they were of the opposite sex.
8. Find at least two people who have broken away from the traditional sex roles in at least one area of their lives.
9. Find three people who have had a female "boss".
10. Find two people who feel the same way you do about female/male roles ...what, if anything they 'should' be.
11. Find two people who felt, when growing up, the same peer group pressure you did regarding sex and sexuality.
12. Find at least three people who recall reading only the 'juicy' parts of certain books when growing up.
13. Find three people who can recall knowing at least one adult female or male when they were growing up who did not fit the traditional model for that person's sex.

# human treasure hunt #4: parenting
## (jim bellanca)

1. Find someone who has adopted a child.
2. Find someone who has strong feelings about how parents can best help kids with sex roles.
3. Find someone who is a single parent.
4. Find someone who believes that "sparing the rod is spoiling the child."
5. Find someone who had good experiences with a child care program.
6. Find someone who is not a parent but has some comments to make about parenting.
7. Find someone who has lost a child through illness or accident.
8. Find someone who is totally absorbed with the parenting role.
9. Find someone who has more than eight children.
10. Find someone who values formal religion in a child rearing process.
11. Find someone who devalues formal religion in the child rearing process.
12. Find someone who is a member of an extended family.
13. Find someone who values the nuclear family.

Ice-breakers can be enjoyable, non-threatening and stimulating ways for you to encourage the people in your group to get to know one another. The mixer games described in this chapter serve as excellent vehicles for groups to build up momentum and energy: when people feel safe and "at home" in a group, they are able to focus attention and energy on the task at hand as well as on building relationships with others in their group.

# 5 intimate and family

Everybody knows the old saying, "The family that plays together stays together" — but is it really true? And if so, what kinds of games should a family be playing together? Certainly not the traditional competitive games that have winners and losers and create sibling rivalries and point out the skills differences between the generations. Well ... what, then?

We have included in this chapter a series of games which encourage playful family interaction and at the same time bring the family closer together, both emotionally and physically. By "families" we mean any intimate group in a supportive relationship — parents and children, two lovers, a communal household, or any number of other combinations and permutations of

# games

loving people. The age or size of a family are not the determining factors. It is the underlying bond of love that makes a group of people a "family unit." There are no limitations to the size of a family that can play together, either — members of the Playfair staff have facilitated giant group play experiences for entire family clans, numbering in the hundreds of relatives, at weddings, wedding anniversaries, birthday parties, and bar mitzvahs. On the other hand, many a larger family has had its start with two lovers playing cooperative games by the fireside!

Although this chapter has been specifically structured to give ideas for family games, many of the other games in this book are appropriate for families as well. There are many different modes in which family members can play together: active physical interactions, quiet reflective ones, creative ones, nurturing sharing times — and we've included examples of all of these throughout this book. The "Mind Games" Chapter, for example, can provide endless evenings of challenging family entertainment, and can transform the nature of a rainy Sunday afternoon. And the game SAFARI from that section

has been known to turn an ordinary outing in the family car into a true journey into the far reaches of the creative mind. Similarly, many of the physically active games like ROLL-PLAYING, MOONWALK, and OFF BALANCE can be played by an entire family together, regardless of physical or age differences. Games like THE HUMAN TABLEAUX from the "Learning Games" chapter can enable players to share some information from their personal histories that even the most intimate of family members may not know. And, when used as a daily evening ritual, an exercise like HIGHLIGHTS WITH PUNCTUATION from the "Endings" chapter is a high-spirited way family members can share the events of the day with each other before sitting down to the evening meal!

---

*For me, playing is loving and loving is playing. It is important to me to play with people who are important to me . . . it's a wonderful way of getting to know another person more deeply.*

---

Cooperative play experiences are especially important for family members to experience together — this is one area where Life can imitate Play. If the skills of cooperative play can be translated into the skills of cooperative life, the family living situation can become more meaningful, growthful, and joyful for all the family members.

*Peerness and mutuality in a play or work relationship can lead to trust, which, in turn, can lead to "being yourself."*

We do not mean to imply that competitive play experiences are never appropriate for family-play situations, or that the games in this book are intended to be a total repertoire of family games. Rather, we hope that these games will give the players a method for transforming traditional, toxic competitive games into a more human-oriented format for playing together.

Too often in competitive family games the players must betray their own integrity in order to "protect" their loved ones from the "agony of defeat." All of us are familiar with . . . the wife who secretly double-faults to avoid winning the set from her husband . . . the husband who plays at half-strength to "make things easy" for his wife . . . the teenage son who carries his father a few minutes in their friendly arm wrestling instead of pinning him immediately . . . the cagey grandfather who sets himself up to be checkmated by his granddaughter. All of these are unselfish gestures, intended to avoid family strife. Yet how much easier it would be if instead families could play *cooperative* games together, in which each player contributes according to his/her full strength, and no one need be afraid of hurting the other players!

The authors of this book are both excellent competitors, both used to winning in most games we play. In fact, we credit the beginning of our friendship to our mutual love of basketball — a quite competitive game! While we were in graduate school Joel gave Matt a lift home from class one day. Matt spied a basketball in the back seat of the car . . . and the rest is history. Weekly games followed, we got to know each other quite well, and a long-term personal and professional friendship was born. We still play basketball whenever we get together, and our shoot-out at Joel's weekend wedding was one of the many highlights of that celebration for both of us!

When we get together to play we face the same dilemma that many family members face in playing together — we both want to do our best, and yet neither of us wants the other to lose. "What's the big deal?" some readers may be asking, "It's only a game!" Quite true, but in the heat of a competitive play situation that fact is often quite difficult to remember. The problem is that many players find their self-concept tied up to the outcome of the game. Every game is a test of their self-worth, and they take defeat in the game as a personal failure as well.

*Unconditional acceptance is at the foundation of any good relationship. It would be nice to have games in which people are accepted for who they are, not what they do.*

One solution that works for us is to build into our games new rules that help us see a clear separation between our relationship as rival players and our relationship as loving human beings. In tennis, for example, as we approach the net to change sides after every odd-numbered game, we stop, hug, and share one thing we like about each other. Then we return to the game and give it all we've got, secure in the knowledge that our close friendship has nothing to do with the outcome. Thus Joel can lose a set six-love and still feel loved; or he can score fifteen straight jump shots and not have to worry about whether Matt will ever talk to him again. Every family is different, of course — and the solution we have found for ourselves may not be appropriate for you. Every family can find its own way of reminding players that "It's only a game," and that the intention of every game — whether it be a cooperative or a competitive one — can be to increase the joy and communication and good feelings between the players.

A number of the games in this "Intimate and Family Games" chapter serve a function that is particularly appropriate here: they promote a new kind of approach to physical touching. As we have facilitated playfulness experiences for hundreds of thousands of adults across the United States, it has become clear to us that we are a nation that is quite literally "out of touch" with itself. Most of us are adequately touched and caressed as infants, but as we grow older there are fewer and fewer socially acceptable avenues by which we can receive supportive physical contact. The family is the place where most of us learn about the boundaries of touching, when it is acceptable and when it is not. Our hope is that through playing games like these within the family unit, families will have some tools for becoming physically closer and more open with each other. As a bonus, younger family members will receive a clear message that touching is OK — and they will grow into adulthood with a better opportunity to create a society in which healthy, supportive touching is the norm.

*Games that use the common sense — of touch — are the ones that "grab me."*

Too often we hear of young adults who turn to sexual contact because it is the only way they can get the physical touching they need. That kind of sexual touching is *not* what these games are about — we are not interested in promoting family orgies — quite the contrary, in fact. You will notice in some of the ''Directions To The Players'' we suggest that the play-facilitators explicitly move these games away from the area of sexual contact. These games are designed to promote sensitivity, open communication, and physical tuning-in to the other players. That can have a long-range effect on all the ways that we touch each other, including the sexual ones.

In short, we hope that the use of these games will contribute to making it easier and more socially acceptable for Americans to begin physically touching each other more frequently and in a more sensitive and a more caring manner.

Although the games in this chapter seem to us particularly appropriate for family use, most of them can also be used quite successfully in other open-ended play situations. Therefore the ''Directions to the Players'' have not been written exclusively for use by family groups, so they may easily be used in any general playgroup situation. Included are:

**wrist dancing**
**finger dancing**
**pleasant memories of childhood**
**  play**
**how to start an argument**
**rebound**
**songs by syllables**
**bouncing the person**
**floating on the ocean**
**flying back stretch**
**octopus massage**
**i love ya honey, but i just can't**
**  make ya smile**

# wrist dancing

Directions to the Players: **Imagine that you have won an all-expenses-paid vacation to New York or to San Francisco. Decide which city you'd rather go to . . . Now pair up with one other member of the group who has made the same choice you have have** . . .

**We're going to do a dance now, in which you will slowly fall away from your partner, then gently catch each other and pull each other back to standing. . . . Start by standing about an arm's length apart, then both lean gently backwards, lose your balance slightly, then reach out and catch each other. Go slowly at first . . . Try to find as many different parts of your arms as you can with which to catch each other — your wrists, the sides of your hands, your forearms, your elbows, your thumbs. It's a very gentle dance, and you and your**

**partner can find your own personal rhythm for your falling away from each other and catching and moving back together. You might want to try it sometimes with both arms, sometimes with one arm, sometimes with the other arm** . . . .

**Comments:** WRIST DANCING is an excellent follow-up exercise to THE HUMAN SPRING (Chapter 3). Physically the two games are exact opposites, and many play group leaders like to have the same pair of partners play together in both games.

A number of the activities in this chapter are based on exercises we learned from teachers of Contact Improvisation, a duet dance form that emphasizes cooperation and trust between the dancers. See "Resources" (Chapter 14) for further information about Contact Improvisation.

# finger dancing

Directions to the Players: **Let's each join up with one other member of the group — perhaps someone you haven't spent much time with yet today ... Stand a few feet away from your partner, facing each other, with your hands at your sides and your eyes closed. Try to sense that other person across from you, tune into his or her breathing, make a silent connection ...**

**Very slowly, let the index finger on one of your hands move up into the space between you and your partner and let it move around in that space until it comes into contact with your partner's index finger. When that happens, let your two fingers fuse together and be still together.**

**Lean slightly into your fingers right now, put a bit of pressure on them. In your mind's eye, take a step back from those two fingers, disconnect yourself from them, watch them as if they existed independently of the two of you. Think of it as if you are holding onto a divining rod which is seeking water — those fingers** have a life of their own, a movement of their own ...

**Now those two fingers begin to move together, but neither of you is controlling them, the impulse to move comes from the fingers themselves. Sometimes it's a subtle, little movement and sometimes it's a big movement, but always the movement comes from the fingers themselves. Follow the motion of the fingers with your body if you have to, explore different levels, high and low. If you find that you're moving around quite a bit, having to take steps to follow your fingers, then open your eyes but don't focus them on your partner or on anything at all in particular. Just use your vision to keep from crashing into anyone ... Sometimes your fingers will come to a resting place together. Allow them to do that, and the next time it happens, allow your fingers to say goodbye and to part from each other ... Open your eyes and tell your partner what you liked about dancing with him/her.**

**Comments:** Many people who have internalized that famous vulture, "Oh, I can't dance — not *me*!" have found in FINGER DANCING that they *can* actually dance with another person. FINGER DANCING is different from the kind of dancing that has vulturized so many of us — it requires no previous study, no fancy steps, no inflexible leading and following. What it requires instead is to merge with one's partner, to flow together, to move together harmoniously, to be sensitive to each other's slightest desires, and to allow the small, minimal movements of one's fingers to express the dancer's spirit within each of us. The smiles of delight and accomplishment that the two partners beam at each other at the end of a shared finger-dance speak eloquently of the joy that creating and physically communicating with another person can bring.

"Tell your partner what you like about . . ." is an instruction that is often useful in ending a playful activity. Most of us have been trained to "criticize" something as soon as it has ended (or even before), and it is rare that we share, instead, what it is that we have enjoyed about an activity or another person. It is obvious that focusing on the positive aspects of the interactions between the players will help to create the atmosphere of cooperation and support that is the basis of a successful non-competitive play experience.

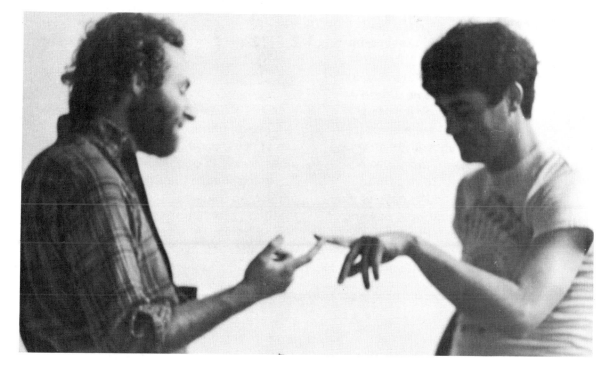

# pleasant memories of childhood play

Directions to the Players: **Please close either your left eye or your right eye . . . . Find one other person who has the same eye closed as you do, and sit down with that person as your partner . . .**

When people get together to try to play supportively after many years of playing — and living — competitively, it can be helpful to remember the times when playing was the central focus of your life. As a child, you make most of your friends by playing with them, and the people you enjoy playing with the most are the people you stay friends with the longest. I'm talking now about growing up playful before the age of ten. Remember that each of us has our own special personal history of the playful side of ourselves. Even two members of the same family, will have entirely different histories of growing up playful.

In a few minutes I'm going to ask you and your partner to share some pleasant memories of your own personal history of your playful past. First let me emphasize that you should really concentrate on trying to remember only *pleasant* memories of being playful. Many of us have painful physical memories of our early days of play — maybe the first time you went bowling you dropped the bowling ball on your foot, or your best friend when you were six once smashed you over the head with a tennis racquet. Well, forget about stuff like that for now.

The idea of this sharing is for you to reconnect with times in your life when you really enjoyed playing.

Okay, it's time for you and your partner to make an important decision now. Would one of you decide to be Eggplant, and the other decide to be Zucchini Squash?... I'm going to give the Eggplants two minutes to think out loud what it was like for them, pleasant memories of growing up playful before the age of ten. Now Eggplants, you might want to start as early as possible and work your way forward.

Maybe there's an incredible memory you have of picking up your rattle and rocking around the crib — or you might want to start later in life than that. Or you might want to spend the whole time thinking about one particular incident, maybe a memory you have of playing jumprope when you were seven. It might be helpful to remember who your playmates were, how you used to dress, where it was that you used to play.

Zucchinis, what I want you to do is to give the Eggplants lots of attention, listen very carefully to them — but don't say anything at all! That's not easy to do. But, don't just sit there and be a stonewall either — give them plenty of support without words. Even if it turns out that you're the long-lost friend who once hit him or her over the head with a tennis racquet — SAY NOTHING! You'll get your chance to talk later, because after two minutes we're going to switch roles.

There's a reason for all this, Zucchinis. When you talk with someone, your mind may be racing to say something intelligent to them, so you hardly take time to listen to them before you start impressing them with your own story — "Oh yeah, the same thing happened to me, only twice as good" — you know, that sort of thing. So this game will give you the chance to really listen deeply to your partner without having to think about what you're going to say back.

One last word of advice to the Eggplants. Don't worry if you run out of things to say. Two minutes is a long time, and it's not a subject you've thought about in a while. So if you have a minute of recalling memories and then half a minute of silence, that's fine. Don't start talking back and forth with that Zucchini. Just take the time silently for yourself, and if something else pops into your head, fine, share it then . . . .

**Comments:** There are many different uses for this structured sharing of pleasant memories. In the example above it is used to help create a frame of mind that will be conducive to the formation of a supportive play community. It's included in this chapter because it is also an excellent way for family members to create a relaxed frame of mind. (In fact many people have reported success in curing headaches by taking some time out to recall pleasant memories).

Sharing pleasant memories other than those of childhood play can also promote relaxation. For example, the Eggplant could ask her partner to "tell me some pleasant memories you have of being by a lake" (or the mountains, or the ocean, or Halloween, or whatever you can think of until you hit one that your partner can relate to). Two to ten minutes is the general time limit we have used for each person to share his/her memories, but it can, of course, be much longer. As in the example above, after a given time limit the two partners switch roles of listener and responder.

Classroom teachers can think of all sorts of sharing that they can do with their students using this sharing in pairs. Some examples: sharing pleasant memories of good times with your family, good times you've had with animals, times that you were excited, pleasant memories about school.

When working with adults, sharing pleasant memories of childhood adventures is an excellent way to get people to meet each other without allowing them to ''pull rank'' on each other. Many adults who are first getting together are very concerned to sniff out each other's relative status, to exchange success stories, to establish some sort of pecking order. But most of us have had relatively similar childhood play experiences, and in talking about this aspect of our childhoods we can meet on a basis of relative equality and shared human experience.

We've found this especially helpful when doing a PLAYFAIR at New Student Orientation at colleges — it gives the Dean of Students and an incoming student a chance to have a meaningful exchange as absolute equals. We also make sure to have a number of childhood sharings when we're working with an office staff that has a rigid and firmly entrenched hierarchy. Sharing childhood memories gives people a glimpse at the real human being behind ''Take a letter!'' and ''yesma'am, Noma'am! Yessir, nosir!''

This is especially true of family members. Children are invariably interested in hearing about their parents' childhood experiences, and the special structure provided by PLEASANT MEMORIES provides a unique opportunity for parents and children to share a discussion with absolute equality in terms of their experience of the subject matter.

PLEASANT MEMORIES is also a great way to pass the time and get to know a group of strangers if, for example, you're taking a long car-ride with a group of people you don't know very well. How much deeper your connection with them can be at the journey's end if you talk about pleasant memories you have of being at the seashore, preparing a special meal, or even of your business life, rather than about the football season, the weather, the latest movies or the presidential election.

This activity is adapted from the work of Re-evaluation Counseling. For more information on this form of peer counseling, see ''Resources,'' Chapter 14.

# how to start an argument

Directions to the Players: **Would you put either your pinky or your thumb into the air ... find one other person who is doing the same thing you are, and sit down with that person as your partner ... You'll get to play this game with your partner in a little while, but first let's go through it together ... Whatever I say, I want you to say the opposite, very forcefully. Ready ... "Yes! (NO!) Yes! (NO!) Yes! (NO!) ... Down! (UP!) Down! (UP!) Down! (UP!) Up! (DOWN!)"** ... Okay, let's up the ante and try it with two words. **"It's Hot! (IT'S COLD!) It's Hot! (IT'S COLD!) It's Hot! (IT'S COLD!)"** ... When you play this game with your partners, you're going to start softly, get louder and louder, and then bring it back on down to soft again. So let's try that: **"loud! (soft!) Loud! (Soft!) LOud! (SOft!) LOUd! (SOFt!) LOUD! (SOFT!) LOUd! (SOFt!) LOud! (SOft!) Loud! (Soft!) loud! (soft!)"** ...

Decide with your partner which of you is going to be Tomato and which is going to be Cucumber ... I would like the Tomatoes to begin the argument, and Cucumbers, say the opposite of what your Tomato partner is saying. Be very forceful about your point of view. The only rule is that you cannot use either the word "I" or the word "You" in your argument.

So Tomatoes, start soft and work your way louder, and then back to softer again.

Cucumbers, argue at exactly the same volume as your Tomato, getting louder when he or she gets louder and softer when he or she gets softer. After you've finished the first word or phrase, Tomatoes, then start again with another word or phrase, and after a while we'll switch roles so the Cucumbers will be starting out a crescendo and the Tomatoes will be arguing with them.

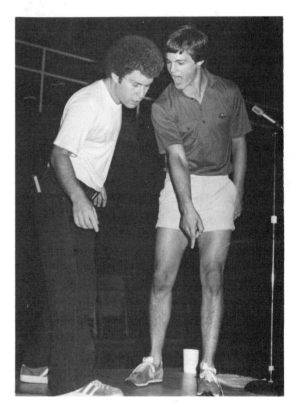

One other thing you both might try is to have a little hand motion to go along to emphasize your word or phrase. Let that hand motion get bigger and bigger as you get louder and louder, and let it get smaller and smaller as you get softer and softer . . . You can play standing up or sitting down. Ready? Let's argue! . . .

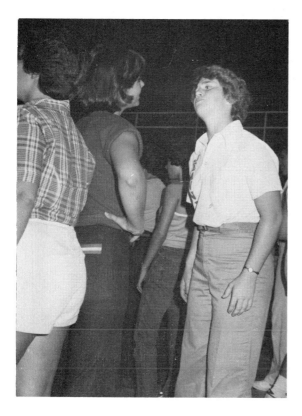

**Comments:** HOW TO START AN ARGUMENT provides a useful structure for family members, because it allows them to argue together in a safe way. The game provides an outlet for angry feelings the players may be carrying around with them, but that they have no way to release without "hurting" someone.

Conflicts, disagreements, and angry feelings are a natural part of any family living situation. The question is, what is the appropriate form in which to exhibit those feelings? HOW TO START AN ARGUMENT can provide a way to play around with feelings of anger, to legitimize their existence, and at the same time to defuse them. When conflicts do arise the family members may be better at dealing with them in a rational and compassionate (rather than in a screaming and door-slamming) manner.

We often end this activity by asking the partners to "make up and tell your partner you didn't really mean it after all," and people have a lot of fun with mock-apologies, forgiving and embracing each other.

The reason for the rule that the players can't use "I" or "You" in their arguments is to prevent scenes like this:

"You're beautiful!"
"I'm Ugly!"
"No, You're beautiful!"
"No, I'm Ugly!" . . .

# rebound

Directions to the Players: **Are you a ping pong ball, or a ping pong paddle? . . . Find a partner who made the same choice — balls find balls, paddles find paddles . . .**

**Stand facing your partner, and now decide which of you is going to choose Hamburger and which is going to choose Soyburger . . . REBOUND is a game of** *action* **and** *response* **. The Hamburgers will start the action at first, and the Soyburgers will be responding; then we'll switch the parts and the Soyburgers will do the initiating and Hamburgers responding . . . Okay? . . . Hamburgers, begin a sound and motion that you can repeat over and over, and direct it toward your partner. Try to convey some sort of emotion in your sound and gesture. It can be a realistic combination, like a person who's laughing and holding her stomach, or like someone who's punching and shouting; or it can be an abstract sound and motion like jumping and saying "ooh" . . . Okay, hamburgers, just keep repeating them over and over at your own rhythm . . .**

**Now, Soyburgers, what I want you to do is to pay careful attention to what the Hamburgers are doing, try to tune into your partner's rhythm . . . Begin to respond to his or her sound-and-motion with a sound-and-motion of your own — a response to what your partner is doing. So they are doing something, and then you are** rebounding to what they are doing by making a sound and motion of your own. And then they do the same thing again, and you respond to it in exactly the same way again, and you are alternating back and forth, back and forth, with your sounds and motions . . .

After a while I want the Hamburgers to stop, while the Soyburgers keep doing their sound-and-motion in the same rhythm. Tune into your partner's rhythm, Hamburgers . . . then rebound to their sound-and-motion with a *new* sound-and-motion of your own, one that is some kind of a response to what your Soyburger is doing. Remember to keep making sounds, both of you, along with your motions . . . Keep alternating back and forth, repeating those same two things, with the Hamburgers rebounding to the Soyburgers' sound-and-motion . . . After a while, Soyburgers, you stop while the Hamburgers keep going . . . Soyburgers, tune into your partner's rhythm again and then rebound to your partner's sound-and-motion . . .

Let's keep alternating back and forth like that, with one of you being the initiator and the other rebounding to you, and then the initiator stopping for a while and then rebounding to the rebound . . .

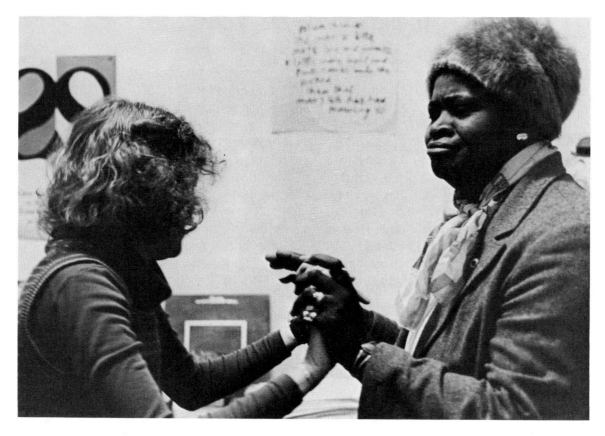

**Comments:** The rhythm of REBOUND is sometimes difficult for players to grasp the first time around (initiate . . . wait and tune in . . . rebound . . .). So it is often useful when introducing this game to do a demonstration with two players in front of the family or group, and to "talk them through" the sequence. The easiest demonstration is a "realistic" one: one player throwing an imaginary ball at another, or blowing a kiss at another, with an appropriate sound done simultaneously . . . and then their partner rebounding to that overt gesture and sound.

The transformations in mood and gesture that the two players go through in a REBOUND sequence can be hilarious. Players who have mastered HOW TO START AN ARGUMENT and CRESCENDO have a good grounding for the complex structure of REBOUND.

We learned REBOUND from George Morrison, an innovative master of Theater Games.

# songs by syllables

Directions to the Players: **Are you wearing a belt? ... Get together with two other people who, like you, are or are not wearing a belt ...**

**This is called SONGS BY SYLLABLES and the first thing we are going to do is to pick a song that we all know. (How about "Row, Row, Row Your Boat"). Okay, what we are going to do is we are each going to sing one syllable at a time of "Row, Row, Row Your Boat," alternating back and forth, and keeping up the rhythm so that it sounds like one voice singing it. Let's give it a try.**

Alvin:     **Row**
Barbara: **Row**
Calvin:   **Row**
Alvin:     **Your**
Barbara: **Boat ...**
Calvin:   **Gent-**
Alvin:     **-ly**
Calvin:   **Down**
Barbara: **The**
Calvin:   **Stream ...**
Alvin:     **Mer-**
Barbara: **-ri**
Calvin:   **-ly ...**

**Got the idea? ... Okay, pick a song with your partners and sing it through a couple of times, then move on to another one you all know.**

**Comments:** Even the most familiar song is a new challenge when it is sung this way. This is a wonderful activity for literally "tuning-in" the players to each other, as they make cooperative decisions together and make mutual adjustments to each other's vocal ranges. It also provides an opportunity for much shared laughter!

This is another game that helps to combat the vultures many of us carry inside us that say "You can't sing!" Because it is a cooperative effort, because the singing is done in such an unusual framework, and because most groups choose very simple nursery-rhyme type songs to sing together, many self-proclaimed "non-singers" do not find SONGS BY SYLLABLES to be a threatening activity. To minimize the possible threat, however, we often preceed it by one of the more "safe" singing games like CHORALE OF THE VOWELS, HUMDINGER or SIMULTANEOUS SONGS.

# bouncing the person

Directions to the Players: **Choose a partner who has a different favorite food than you ... Decide with your partner which of you is going to be Rabbit, and which is going to be Ostrich ... Would the Rabbits raise your left hand? Would the Ostriches raise your right foot? Okay, put them down.**

**We're going to do a very subtle little activity called BOUNCING THE PERSON. The Rabbits are going to be bounced first and the Ostriches are going to do the bouncing; then we'll reverse roles. But don't worry, we're not going to turn you into a rubber ball and bounce you all over the place — it's a much more gentle, soothing type of bounce.**

**Okay Rabbits, what I would like you to do is to close your eyes and relax, hands down at your sides, listen to your breathing ... feel yourself relaxing, but at the same time keep yourself erect, so that you're not slumped over ... Ostriches, place the palm of one of your hands very lightly on the top of your Rabbit-partner's head. This is the hand that is going to help with the bouncing, but in fact you're hardly going to move it at all. What I want you to do now is to *think* about your arm getting heavy ... send some heavy-weight energy down through the palm of your hand, through the head and down the spine of your partner.**

**The Rabbits are going to tune into that energy and it's going to press them ever so slightly down into the bottom of their spines, so they sink down a bit with the heaviness of that energy ... Okay Ostriches, now think *light* into your arm ... the energy that you're centering in your palm is moving up now instead of down, and the Rabbits, as they sense it, are going to be pulled slightly up towards that energy source ... It's a very slight movement, an expanding up at the top of the spine, stretching the head upwards ... Okay Ostriches, you're on your own now, find your own rhythm and your own balance ... alternate slowly between down energy and up energy, very gently and subtly bouncing up and down your Rabbit partner. After a few minutes we'll reverse the roles ...**

**Comments:** We particularly like this activity because of the opportunity it gives the partners to pay attention sensitively to each other. Being ''bounced'' is a soothing, relaxing, and centering experience, and we often use it to allow the members of a group to re-focus their concentration after a madcap experience like ANIMALS or one of the other high-energy games.

BOUNCING THE PERSON and the three games that follow can be used in sequence by family members to promote a sense of relaxation, group nurturing, and physical closeness with each other.

# floating on the ocean

Directions to the Players: **Get together in a group of three . . . decide which one of you is going to be Submarine, which is going to be Sailboat, and which is going to be Ocean Liner . . .**

We're going to do a group relaxation fantasy together about floating on a raft in the middle of the ocean. The Submarines are going to get relaxed first, and the two partners will assist, then we'll rotate around. So Submarines, the first thing I want you to do is stand with your feet together and your hands hanging loosely at your sides . . . Take a deep breath and hold it, and as you exhale it let your eyes close and let your body relax . . . imagine yourself floating on a raft in the middle of the ocean . . . To heighten the fantasy for you, imagine you hear the waves breaking on the shore way in the distance. Listen to those waves, and feel yourself floating on the ocean, totally safe, totally taken care of . . .

Sailboats and Liners, stand directly behind your Submarine now and put one hand on her shoulder and one hand on the small of her back . . . Begin rocking her weight very gently now, back on her heels, then forward to standing balance again, rocking her back and forth in time to the waves . . . Since her eyes are closed and her heels are together, even a slight rocking motion like that seems like a big motion to her — you don't have to bring her down to the floor and then back up again . . . Very slowly now finish your rocking, and bring her to complete standing balance, and when you're sure that she can stand by herself, very very slowly take away your hands, so slowly that she can't quite tell when you're not touching her any longer . . . And now Submarine would you slowly open your eyes and come back to the room and thank your partners for that gift . . .

Now in each group we'll go on to the Ocean Liners, and then to the Sailboats. So Ocean Liners, stand with your feet together and your hands at your sides, and take a deep breath and hold it . . .

**Comments:** FLOATING ON THE OCEAN is closely related to BOUNCING THE PERSON. Because it is a less subtle experience, we often use it instead of BOUNCING THE PERSON with more "resistant" groups. FLOATING ON THE OCEAN gives players the feeling of physically supporting each other and of taking a physical risk with their bodies, but it is in actuality less dangerous than many other "trust" games.

If you want to give the participants the sound of the seashore in the background in order to heighten the fantasy, we would recommend the record "Environments 1: The Psychologically Ultimate Seashore." (Atlantic Records).

We have received mixed feedback from the players when we asked them about the amount of side-coaching to be done by the group leader during the course of this exercise. Some participants said that it helped them when the group leader was silent for a few moments and the participants could tune-in to the sound of the distant waves. Other participants shared that having the facilitator's voice constantly and reassuringly intoning things like "You are getting more and more relaxed . . . you feel safer than you've ever felt in your life" . . . was a great help to them. Other professionals who do systematic relaxation training report similar differences. Play leaders will need to try out their own styles and determine what is most appropriate for each individual group.

# flying back stretch

Directions to the Players: **Find a partner about the same size as you** . . . sit down with that person . . . Decide which of you is going to be apple and which is going to be orange . . . Okay, you and your partner get up and find another pair, so now you're a foursome . . .

We're going to do something called the FLYING BACK STRETCH. You're going to get a totally-supported chance to really stretch out your back and let out some of the tension you may be storing in there. You're going to be supported by the back of your partner and by the arms of the other partners. It's a fabulous feeling, like flying through the air.

If anyone here has a history of back trouble, now is the time to say so — don't do this if you think it might be harmful to you. That's a really important thing to learn — take care of yourself, don't do anything *you* don't want to do. At the same time, be sure you are there to support the other people in what they want to do.

Let's have the apples go first. Would one of the apple-orange pairs stand back-to-back and link arms? Now pair number two stand on either side of them . . . Orange number one, I want you to bend slightly at the knees, so your center of balance is lower than your partner's — and the second pair, put your hands on apple number one's hips, to help guide her

. . . Apple, lean back into your partner now and start to give your weight to him, and Orange, you begin to bend over forward and lift your partner onto your back . . . Notice he is not lifting the apple with the strength of his arms, but with his hips and pelvis. Good! And the other pair is helping the Apple keep her balance up there, supporting her gently . . .

Apple, really let yourself relax into it and be supported, and feel that stretch. I'd like you and your Orange to unlink your arms, and Apple, let your arms stretch way out over your head. How are you doing down there, Orange? If you feel any strain at all — and this goes for everybody when you're in that supporting position — say so right away, and we'll lower the Apple to the ground slowly. Don't ever strain yourself down there. Are you getting a good massage on your back down there, Orange? Good!

I'd like the two supporting people to slowly let go of the Apple now so she's really floating free, but be there to support her in case she starts to lose her balance. Let yourself stretch all the way out, and shift your weight around if you want to, Apple, whatever feels best to you, so long as Orange is okay . . . Now let's begin to lower the Apple back down to the ground slowly. Would you grasp her around the hips, Orange, and the two support-persons hold her there too . . . **Now Apple, let yourself be lifted to standing — you're not going to do any of the work yourself . . . Okay Orange, slowly begin to bring yourself upright, and support the Apple all the way — don't pull yourself up, Apple, let the Orange bring you to standing. Steady her there . . . Apple, tell your partners how it was for you!** . . .

**Let me talk everybody through it the same way. We'll begin again with the second Apple being supported by his or her Orange partner** . . .

**Comments:** FLYING BACK STRETCH is the activity in this book that has the greatest possibility of being "dangerous," so the safety factor cannot be stressed too strongly.

The smaller the group you are working with (so you can give personal attention to everyone) the better. In a family, you probably know the limits of each person. In general, the greater the size of the participants, the greater the possibility of injury — two 100-pound people can support each other's weight a lot more easily than two 200-pound people can.

If you are working with a fairly large group it is possible that some of the participants will feel hesitant about allowing themselves to be lifted up into the air. That's fine, and you should certainly give them the option of passing when it is their turn to be lifted into the air. However, it is important that, although they may not want to be lifted into the air themselves, all the participants contribute fully to physically supporting the players who do want to experience the FLYING BACK STRETCH.

# octopus massage

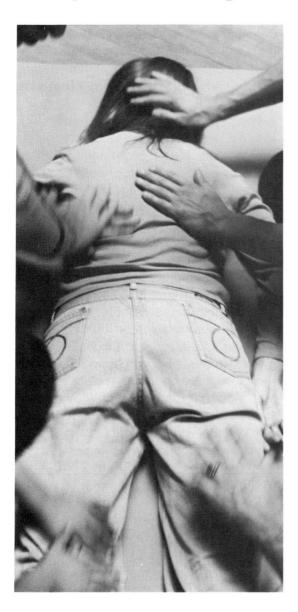

Directions to the Players: **We're going to give ourselves a real treat now. Would you form a group with four others\* who are wearing at least one item of the same color as something you have on?** ... **Each of us is going to take turns being massaged by the others in our group. Let's start with the oldest person in the group, then everyone else will get a turn too.** Okay, oldest person, would you lie face down on the floor? ... **The rest of us sit around her** ... **I'm going to start leading, massaging her and my three partners are going to follow my lead, doing exactly what I do on different parts of her body at the same time. We might start off rubbing her gently and strongly** ... **then switch to a gentle-but-firm slapping, pounding rhythm** ... **and then to a much lighter stroke** ...

**All the time we'll be watching her reactions, and making sure that we're not tickling her or doing something that's unpleasant for her — after all, each person is different, and we want to make sure that we're doing something** *good* **for her! I want to make it clear also that this is not a time to start coming-on sexually to the person you're massaging, either. Your job is to** *serve* **that person, to** *take care* **of her or him, to make things as comfortable as possible.**

---

*Smaller groups are ok. See "Comments"

All of the groups will be doing their massages simultaneously, and after a minute has passed I'll call time and we'll all stop at the same time. Then a new person will take his or her place in the center, we'll switch to a new leader and rotate to a different position around the new body, and massage that second person for a minute as well. At least once during the course of the massage, let's make an agreement that each leader will lead us in vigorous, pounding-but-not-hurtful-cascade for at least ten seconds . . .

**Comments:** It's easy to see why this is called the OCTOPUS MASSAGE — feeling those eight hands working on you is quite an extraordinary experience! Of course if your family or group has fewer than five persons, it's still possible to have an effective group massage using this method. The main things to remember are to give each person equal time in the center, and to allow the rest of the group to work together as a unit to "serve" the person who is being massaged. The object of the leader in each group is not to show off all the clever massage variations that s/he can think of, but to coordinate the group effort by sensitively tuning into the responses of the person being massaged.

As is the case with FLYING BACK STRETCH, it is possible that some of the participants in a large group will feel shy about being massaged. We suggest giving them the option of declining to receive the massage, while remaining actively involved in giving the massage to the other players.

# i love ya honey, but i just can't make ya smile

Directions to the Players: **If the name of this game, I LOVE YA HONEY, BUT I JUST CAN'T MAKE YA SMILE, is any indication (and it is), you know that this is going to be a fun-tabulous game! What we need to do first is to form a seated-circle, so pull up your chair, or pull up your floor, and get into a circle .... Okay, now that I have a circle under my eyes, we can begin.**

**One person starts off as the center person. For demonstration purposes — and because I really dig it! — I'll begin as the center person. I need to locate the lap of one person in the circle, and plop myself down in that person's lap ... Okay, now that I am in lap-land, I say those immortal (not immoral!) words, "I love ya honey, but I just can't make ya smile." Of course, my objective is to say it in such a way that the person will break into uncontrollable laughter, or at the very least, crack a tiny Mona Lisa smile. Now, when I'm in your lap, try as hard as you can not to crack a smile. If you do, then you take my place as center person, find someone else's lap to sit on, and repeat those memorable words ... Feel free to be creative and experiment with different intonations and gestures and ways of communicating "I love ya honey, but I just can't make ya smile." Let the hambone in you tickle the funnybone of your lap-mate. At the same time, be** respectful of the person whose lap you're occupying. "Plop down" with care.

**Any questions?... Okay, who would like to be the center person?... All hams on deck!... Start us off!...**
Comments: I LOVE YA HONEY, BUT I JUST CAN'T MAKE YA SMILE provides an opportunity to legitimize laughter, smiling, and humor by coming in the back door — by saying that the object of the game is *not* to smile, *not* to laugh. It's a lot of fun for the participants to play around with something that is "forbidden" — since often one of the great joys of childhood is to do something that is a no-no.

We'll sometimes add a guideline to the game: namely, that a center person is limited to two laps — after that s/he must take a seat in the circle, and the second person whose lap s/he occupied now becomes the center person. This keeps the game moving, and avoids having one person "stuck" in the center for the whole game (sometimes, the center person really laps up all the attention that comes her/his way). It also affords the players a chance to see how different people tackle the same problem — there are many creative, dramatic alternative ways of saying "I love ya honey, but I just can't make ya smile."

Thanks to Margie Ingram, who made us smile when she taught us this game.

The games described in this chapter suggest that the family that plays together will "work" together. Cooperation in play can carry over into other aspects of family life, building a dynamic "team spirit" and sense of caring among the individual family members. Cooperative games can also be used to promote more awareness and joy in reaching out and touching one another — literally and figuratively. We encourage you to springboard off the games in this chapter and develop your own approaches to "getting in touch" with those who are closest to you!

# 6 energizers: what to do when 7:30 sharp and end at 10:30 dull

It's Monday morning, and the people in your office need a "shot in the arm" to help get them going for the week ... It's Thursday afternoon and the students in your class seem restless and unable to pay attention ... It's Friday night and your parents have just come home from work — exhausted ... It's Wednesday morning, and your group seems to be "asleep at the wheel" while you give a lecture ... It's Sunday night, you're pulling an all-nighter with some friends in order to complete a group project, and you need something to keep you going ... It's Tuesday right after lunch, and the people in your group seem drowsy while you try to get a meeting started ... It's Saturday evening, and you're looking for something fun to do at the not-too-exciting party you're attending.

There are many occasions which call for the use of energizer games. Energizers are direct, efficient, and enjoyable ways to "pick up" you and your group. They enable people to re-charge their batteries

# your meetings start at

and help to add excitement and laughter to parties, classrooms, meetings, and family gatherings. They can be used at the beginning of a session (to get things off the ground), in the middle of a session (to make a transition), and/or at the end of a session (to leave participants with an energizing and positive experience).

A wide variety of energizers appears in this chapter. You'll find games that require little space to do (FOUR UP, SIMULTANEOUS SONGS, THE 39 STEPS); require a fair amount of room to carry out (AMOEBA TAG, TRAIN STATION, GROUP WALK); involve people playing in pairs (BACK TO BACK DANCING, THE 39 STEPS); involve people playing on ''teams'' (GROUP CHEER, LAUGH GAUNTLET, AMOEBA TAG); involve the whole group playing together at once (ROLL PLAYING, GROUP WALK, AMOEBA TAG, TRAIN STATION); are simple (FOUR UP, ROLL PLAYING); are more complicated (SIMULTANEOUS SONGS, GROUP CHEER).

*Someone who gives me ''carte blanche'' — permission to be silly, to be goofy, is the kind of person who liberates my playful self. There can be a lot of sense in non-sense.*

How do you know which energizer(s) to use? The key is to choose one appropriate to your group's needs at a particular time. For instance, if your group is dragging, you might want to pick something that would get people up and moving — literally (such as THE 39 STEPS or FOUR UP). If you sense that fear (of reaching out to others) is what is blocking the group's energy, then you might want to play around with BACK TO BACK DANCING, TRAIN STATION, or AMOEBA TAG. If, on the other hand, your group is ''off the wall'' with too much energy to focus on the task at hand (Friday afternoon in school before a vacation!), then you might prefer to draw on some of the games in the INTIMATE AND FAMILY

GAMES chapter to help people relax
(FINGER DANCING, BOUNCING THE
PERSON, FLOATING ON THE OCEAN).

We hope the games in this chapter will
energize you to create your own. Many
teachers and group leaders we have
worked with have found it effective to ask
different members of the group on a
rotating basis to lead energizers .... in
this way, you are sharing responsibility
with others for the energy level of your
group. It can be useful to set up an
"energizers swap shop," in which each
person can share a way to give him/herself
or others a "shot in the arm."

Ready to pick up some energy? In the
pages following you'll find:

**four-up**
**the 39 steps**
**back to back dancing**
**amoeba tag**
**train station**
**groupwalk**
**roll playing**
**laugh gauntlet**
**simultaneous songs**
**group cheer**

Try saying these backwards three times
and see if you're not energized!

# four up

Directions to the Players: **This is a game with very simple rules. We'll start sitting down. Anyone can stand up whenever she or he wants to, but you cannot remain standing for more than five seconds at a time before you sit down again. Then you can get right up again if you want to. Our object as a group is to have exactly four people standing at all times.**

**Comments:** This game focuses each person's attention very carefully on the other members of the group. The game usually lasts about a minute — but what pandemonium and laughter is generated in that minute! When used as a quick break in the middle of a lesson or business meeting or training session where people's attention is beginning to wander, FOUR UP is a splendid energizer. FOUR UP is probably the least threatening activity in this whole book, so it is an excellent game to play with a group who might be resistant to the notion of playing together. FOUR UP introduces them to the idea of playful ''energizer'' breaks in their meetings. If you are going to play this game with more than ten people it is best to play it simultaneously in a number of subgroups with eight people or so in each subgroup.

# the 39 steps

Directions to the Players: **Find a partner whose thumb is just about the same size as yours ... Sit down facing him or her ... I want you to gaze deep into each other's eyes, and on the count of "carrot," I want each of you to call out a number between zero and fifteen ... Ready? ...**

**Rootabaga ... spinach ... lettuce ... carrot! ... Find out what your partner called out and add your numbers together, so you now have a combined number between zero and thirty. Get to your feet and stand back to back with your partner, linking arms ...**

**Now when I say "Kangaroo," I'd like you to take exactly as many jumps into the air, linked together, as the total of your two numbers, combined ... Remember that's a beautiful human body you're holding onto there, and you and your partner want to do this** *together*, **tuned into each other's movements, not having one person dragging the other one all over the place. Okay ... Kangaroo!"**

**Comments:** THE 39 STEPS is an excellent warm-up game early in a play session, because it gets the players laughing, touching each other, moving around, and paying careful attention to each other.

A number of teachers have also told us that they use it as a short break in a long lecture. We heartily endorse the idea of giving students a short physical break in the midst of any sustained mental work — you'll be amazed at how it can improve concentration and the overall classroom atmosphere! Students who get the chance to jump around (or to switch seats with each other, or any other physically-active diversion) invariably have a renewed attention for the "lesson" in progress.

And that is true for adults as well. The next time you're at a meeting and you feel your attention wandering, ask everyone in the room to take exactly 26 hops around the room, and to wind up in a new seat. We guarantee that things will not be the same after that!

It's possible to combine THE 39 STEPS with one of the most famous games invented by The New Games Foundation, "Stand Up." In this variation, the players start by sitting back-to-back on the floor with their arms linked, then attempt to stand up together before taking the prescribed number of jumps. For more information about The New Games Foundation, see "Resources," Chapter 14.

# back to back dancing

Directions to the Players: **Find a partner whose eyes are a different color than yours . . . . Going out dancing is wonderful, but there's one thing wrong with it — you always have to keep your eyes on your partner, and you never get to check out all the other people who are whirling around you on the dance floor. So we're going to do a dance now that is the opposite of that — this time you're going to get to look at everybody** *but* **your own partner!**

**So stand up back-to-back with your partner and link arms with him or her, in just a minute we're going to do a very short dance together, back-to-back. Now, as you're whirling brilliantly across this dance floor here, be sure to take a good look at the other couples whirling by, and give a nice smile of greeting as you catch someone's eye.**

**Of course we have an interesting question to answer here: WHO'S LEADING? Try to make it so that no one's leading, so that you and your partner are flowing harmoniously together, tuning into each other. Remember that is a beautiful human being that you're attached to there, so don't yank each other around the dance floor, or pull each other around the dance floor, but really create a beautiful back-to-back dance together. You might want to sing a little music as you dance together, or you might want to dance together without music . . . Ready? Da, da-da, da-da . . .**

Comments: You might want to play a record in the background (or in the foreground, if you feel like getting a back-to-back disco going). We often end this experience by recommending that the dancers ''thank your partner for that wonderful dance,'' and that simple suggestion usually brings about an explosion of energy, with the partners bowing and curtsying to each other, kissing each other on the hand, and/or embracing each other. Most adults seem to have had a common experience of embarrassment and tension (left over from high-school, perhaps) with ''formal'' dances, and this back-to-back dance seems to give people a chance to laugh at their former up-tightness without bringing up the embarrassing feelings.

We often encourage the dancers to switch partners several times during the course of the dance. This is quite a complicated maneuver when two back-to-back couples try to switch partners with each other by unlinking an arm from the old partner and relinking with the new partner, one arm at a time, *with all four people dancing around the whole while.* The coordination involved in changing partners can be half the fun in this dance! You may want to set a goal, such as "try to dance with at least five other people before this dance is over!"

# train station

Directions to the Players: **Find a partner who identifies with a different cartoon character than you . . . Stand about twenty feet away from your partner, but so you can still maintain eye contact with that person . . . Give your partner a little wave, so you can make sure he can see you. Imagine that your partner is your best friend in the world — from the time that you were both four years old. You haven't seen him since then, but you just got a telegram saying "Meet me at the train station!" . . . So here you are at the train station, the train has just come in, and you are VERY EXCITED! This is your best friend in the world!**

**Now, one thing you have to know is that this whole thing takes place in slow motion.**

**You are going to move towards your partner VERY SLOWLY, waving to him, maybe you're blowing kisses to him, very excited to see that person, ready to embrace him. All in slow motion . . . As soon as you get about two feet away, you realize that IT'S THE WRONG PERSON. Needless to say, you are mortified! You are very embarrassed, so what you do is you pretend that all along you've been waving to** someone behind him. **So you keep on going past your partner, moving slowly towards somebody else, and as soon as you get close to her — the same thing happens again! . . . Okay, begin by waving in slow-motion to your partners — remember you are VERY EXCITED to see them — and go to it . . .**

**Comments:** TRAIN STATION is a useful warm-up for a slow motion tag game like AMOEBA TAG. Because the players are ''acting'' the part of someone who is supposed to be embarrassed, TRAIN STATION gives them permission to do things that are usually too embarrassing in ''real life'' — like waving at strangers, looking people right in the eye, blowing kisses and making other affectionate gestures to the people around them. Lots of good, healthy laughter comes out during this game!

# amoeba tag

Directions to the Players: **This tag game is played entirely in slow motion. Suppose that I am It and I'm chasing after Jamal in slow motion and he's trying to get away in slow motion. At last I catch him. But instead of the It passing from me to Jamal, he and I link arms and become It** *together*. **We are now a "teenage" amoeba on the prowl! When we catch Kenny, he links arms with us, and we are an almost-full-grown amoeba. When the three of us catch Nancy, she also links up with us and we are now a fully mature amoeba. And what happens to a full-grown amoeba? Right! It reproduces by splitting down the middle. So the four of us divide down the middle into two teenage amoebas on the prowl! And then we go our separate ways,**

multiplying and dividing again and again until *everybody* here has been totally amoebafied.

There's one final thing we have to learn before we can start to play, and that's the world-famous Amoeba Chant. It goes like this: A! ME! BA!!! Let's all try it together. (A! ME! BA!!!) Let's try it four times in a row, starting very slowly and then getting louder and louder until the final one is a blood-curdling, giant amoeba-on-the-prowl ("amoeba!" "Amoeba!" "AMOEba!" "AMOEBA!") . . . Now you may well ask, how do we use this fabulous chant? When everyone here has been totally amoebafied — when you are walking around in your two or three person amoeba and all you can see around you are other amoebas on the prowl — then very softly begin the Amoeba Chant. As soon as everybody else hears that chant we'll all join in with it and we'll begin to move together into a giant mass of protoplasm and we'll bring our chant to a final crescendo and that will be the end of this game and we'll move on to the next one.

Okay, let's have two people start as It. Who wants to be It? . . .

**Comments:** There is no limit to the number of people who can play AMOEBA TAG at once. If some strangers have wandered by and are observing your play session, (or if some latecomers are feeling shy about joining the group), having them be "amoebafied" by the other players can be a fun way to get them involved.

For some of the thinking behind the creation of AMOEBA TAG, see Chapter 11, "Inventing Your Own Games."

# groupwalk

Directions to the Players: **Stand up right where you are and close your eyes and listen to what's happening inside you right now ... Bring yourself into a completely centered, evenly-balanced standing position ... Now start swaying slightly left to right ... left ... right ... left, take a step to the left ... and then a step to the right ... left ... right ... let your movements be real rounded and flowing, one step leading right into the next one ... Slowly open your eyes ...**

**Let's start moving around the space now, each of us taking our flowing steps in rhythm with the rest of us ... Keep walking in rhythm with everyone else ... Now let your center of balance be in back of you, so you're leaning backwards, trucking along ... now it's in front of you ... now to the left ... now to the right ... now your center of balance is very low, so you're moving very low to the ground ... now it's very high ...**

**Okay, keep walking and sort of shake yourself out all over as you're moving — we're not trying to move in rhythm with each other anymore. Try to find your natural way of walking, the way you'd normally walk down the street ... You know the way sometimes you're walking home late at night and you're afraid that someone is creeping up right behind you? Well, we're going to really let you get into** that paranoia now, because what I want you to do on occasion is to walk right up behind somebody and see if you can walk exactly as they're walking. Then after you've done that for a while go back to your own normal walk, and then after a while come up behind somebody else and try out their way of walking ...

Keep walking around now, but this time try to walk in a way that is different from the way that you normally walk. You might want to change your center of balance, or the level that you're walking on, or the speed that you move, or all of those. And every once in a while come up beside somebody else and try to take over their walk exactly ...

**Comments:** It's amazing what complex variations there can be in a simple act like walking! Walking together in rhythm gives many people a sense of group unity and connectedness. This activity is a good one to use as a warm-up to TOUCH BLUE, which involves the players calling out movement commands to each other.

# roll-playing

Directions to the Players: **What we're going to be doing now is some roll-playing, but it's going to be different than the kind you've heard about before. The first step is for all of us to sit down on the floor, and form a tight circle, so that you are touching your neighbor on either side. You'll find it helpful to extend your feet into the center of the circle. Okay, let's go do it . . . round 'em up!**

**Okay, now what do we do now that we all have the floor? We're going to have a ball, of course! That is, I will place this basketball on the lap of one person in our circle. The object of the game is to move the ball around our circle as quickly as possible, from lap to lap, without using our hands. Overlapping is encouraged, and may even be necessary! Let's try it . . . .**

**Now that we've got that down pat, let's add a couple of signals to our merry-go-round. Each person in our circle now has a quota of one "reverse" — that is, anyone in the circle can say once during the game "reverse." When we hear that, we need to send the ball in the opposite direction. Okay, let's start the ball circle-lating!**

**Comments:** We've found that this is one game that can leave people literally rolling in the aisles. It's a great deal of fun, and quite a challenge in fact, to keep the ball moving as fast as possible without using your hands. It also requires a great deal of teamwork, cooperation, and sensitivity to the other players.

There are a number of ways to spice up the game even more. One option is to add more signals (for instance, "stop," "go," "slow motion," etc.). Another option is to add more balls. About two minutes into the game, we like to add a smaller ball (like a softball). Two minutes later, you might see what happens if you add a tennis ball to the circle. A golf ball or ping pong ball added to the circle can increase the fun geometrically. The players really have to synchronize with each other's rhythm as they keep the different-sized balls moving around the circle as quickly as possible (and sometimes, different balls are going in different directions)!

# simultaneous songs

Directions to the Players: **Everyone gets a chance to listen to people singing songs on the radio, and lots of us get the chance to sing songs ourselves — whether it's singing together with a group of people, or just singing in the shower. But something that most of us never do is to compose our own song! It's a fabulous experience to sing a song that you've written yourself. This game is called SIMULTANEOUS SONGS, and it's a chance for all of us to compose our own songs and to sing them all at the same time!**

**However if we're all singing different songs at the same time, they all need to have the same tune so it's not total chaos! Let's agree on a familiar tune that we can all sing. Who's got one? ("Mary had a little lamb!") Good. Let's all hum that together. (Dah-da-da-da-dah-dah-dah) ... This is going to be a song in three different verses, to the tune of "Mary Had A Little Lamb." Anyone can call out a topic for the first verse, like "Desserts!" Then that person calls out "1-2-3!" And on "3!" we all sing our own little song about desserts, all of us singing the same tune at the same time, but using different words. So one person might be singing "I like choc-o-late ice-cream!" while someone else might be singing "Fro-zen yo-gurt is the best!" As soon as that's done, somebody calls out the category for the next verse, counts to**

**three, and then we all sing our songs about that subject. When that's done, we go on to the grand finale. So we might wind up singing songs that have three verses: one about dessert, one about polevaulting, and one about polar bears ... Okay? What's our first verse going to be about?**

Comments: Many of us have internalized "vultures" that tell us that we should never sing in public. There are a number of activities in this book that complement SIMULTANEOUS SONGS in providing a safe, supportive atmosphere for the players to rediscover the joys of group singing. HUMDINGER, CHORALE OF THE VOWELS, and SONGS BY SYLLABLES are all distinctive variations on this musical theme.

The combination of harmony/discord/creativity/loud noise/spontaneity makes SIMULTANEOUS SONGS an excellent energizer. It can be especially useful in situations where people do not have an opportunity to move around freely (in a fixed-seat auditorium, in a crowded classroom, in a small family room, on a long bus ride, ...).

# group cheer

Directions to the Players: **What we're going to do right now is to create together our official Group Cheer. The first thing we need is a four-syllable word or phrase, like "Tomato Soup" or "Penicillin." Who's got one? ("Eat your heart out!") Let's all practice that together. (EAT YOUR HEART OUT!!) Okay, who has another one —it doesn't have to have anything to do with the first one. ("Acorn squash!") Acorn squash? That has only three syllables, how can we make it four? ("Squash an acorn!") Fine, Squash an acorn. Let's try both our phrases together. (EAT YOUR HEART OUT! SQUASH AN ACORN!) Who has one more to go with the first two, our grand finale? ("I kissed a fish!") All right, let's put them all together on four. Ready? One, two, three, four — (EAT YOUR HEART OUT! SQUASH AN ACORN! I KISSED A FISH!!)**

**Now, put that incredible cheer away in the back of your mind for a while, and I'm going to ask you a couple of questions. If you have worn a sweater at any time today, raise your hand ... Okay, put 'em down, and remember that you are the Sweater Wearers.**

**Question number two. When you get back to your home tonight, you will find waiting for you either two slightly overweight camels, or six-hundred slightly overripe eggplants. If you would rather**

**sleep with the eggplants, raise your hand right now ... Put your hands down, and remember that you are the Eggplant Sleepers.**

**If you have not raised your hand for either of the two previous questions, raise your hand now ... Okay, we'll call you The Rest of Us.**

**The fourth and last question. Imagine that you have an apple in your left hand and a banana in your right hand. If you would rather eat the banana right now, raise your right hand ... You are the Banana Eaters. So throw the banana over your left shoulder, and throw the apple straight up in the air.**

**I'm going to call out the name of your group and when I call out the name, put your hand up and down real fast. It's possible that you might be in as many as three different groups. Sweater Wearers! ... Eggplant Sleepers! ... The Rest of Us! ... Banana Eaters! ... Let's give each of those groups numbers, so the Sweater Wearers will be number one, the Eggplant Sleepers number two, The Rest of Us number three, and the Banana Eaters number four. When I call out the number of a group that you're in, do the same thing — raise your hand up and down ... 1! 2! 3! 4! ... 1! 2! 3! 4! ...**

**Let's go back to the cheer we invented earlier, "Eat your heart out, Squash an**

acorn, I kissed a fish.'' You'll notice that each of our phrases has four beats or syllables, and that we have four different groups. So we're going to chant our cheer together, and what I want you to do is to raise your hand up and down on the beats that correspond to the group you're in. So suppose that you're in group one and group four, the Sweater Wearers and the Banana Eaters. You'd be chanting the cheer, and you'd be raising your hand up and down on the first and fourth beats of each phrase, Eat . . . Out . . . Squash . . . Corn . . . I . . . Fish. Okay, let's try it. (EAT YOUR HEART OUT! SQUASH AN ACORN! I KISSED A FISH!)

Great! Let's take it one step further now. This time you can only chant when your hand is in the air. So you'll only chant *those* beats of the cheer . . . such as ''Eat . . . Out.'' So, you'll really have to scream it out this time, because there will be fewer people on each syllable. Ready? (EAT YOUR HEART OUT! SQUASH AN ACORN! I KISSED A FISH!)

All right! Now our last and final version, the grand finale. This time instead of raising your hand in the air you're going to jump up in the air in unison with your group, shout out your syllable and sit back down again, getting ready to jump up again when your next group comes around . . . Let's stand up and stretch out legs a bit before we get started . . . Okay, sit down again . . . Ready? Sweater Wearers, you're going to start us off. Got it? Okay, go to it! (EAT YOUR HEART OUT! SQUASH AN ACORN! I KISSED A FISH!)

**Comments:** GROUP CHEER works just as well with the participants sitting in chairs as it does if they are sitting on the floor. So this can be a good game to try with groups who are assembled in a limited physical space like a meeting room or an auditorium. You might find this to be an effective game to use as a follow-up to FOUR UP.

Feel free to adapt the way you introduce this game. For example, some groups may want to start small and work with just one four-syllable cheer (e.g., ''We're fam-i-ly!'') repeated over and over, while other groups may want to be real hot-dogs and start with five cheers (perhaps with the words written down so that everyone can follow them).

Be sure your instructions are understood by your group. Young children for example, may need a simplified version at first.

What a powerful spectacle this can be if there are lots and lots of ''cheerleaders'' leaping into the air and cheering together! The four questions for getting the participants into random groups are obviously flexible (you wouldn't want to ask the one about sweaters in the summer, for example, or you'd have nobody in that group) and you can have a good time making up your own questions to suit your particular group of cheerleaders.

Energy is a valuable — and limitless — resource. The only problem is that sometimes it is hard to find! The games presented in this chapter are designed to tap the human energy resources of the people in your group — whether it be a classroom, a business meeting, a family gathering, or a party. As you'll see in using these games, once you tap one individual's enthusiasm, it's contagious. So if things start to slow down in your group, or if you feel you need a change of pace, call on one or more of the games in this chapter to lift your spirits — and energy level!

# **7**games for learning:
## recess always was the best part of

Mark Twain often joked about his vow never to let his schooling interfere with his education. Unfortunately, the games people play in schools often leave young people (and adults) with no desire to continue learning after the 3 P.M. bell rings. The result is a heavy toll on how people feel about learning itself — many view it as an end-joy, rather than something that they enjoy.

*Having fun and learning are not mutually exclusive.*

Almost all the games in this book have a place in the classroom learning environment: as exercises to promote relaxation, as energizers, or as ways for students to make contact with each other on the feeling/sharing/frolicking level. We are strong believers in the proposition that a "fun" classroom environment is one in which extraordinary learning can take place. In our teaching and lecturing experience it has been demonstrated over

# school!

and over that allowing our listeners repeated breaks from the ''content'' of a session (during which they play one of the PLAYFAIR games) allows them to participate in the content learning with renewed attention and energy.

In that sense this whole book is about ''learning games.'' And not only teachers, but students as well, can institute a ''recharging'' time in classroom lessons, with students themselves leading the class in a series of these cooperative games and exercises.

The specific games in this chapter, therefore, were chosen because they are somewhat different from the rest of the games in this book. These ''learning games'' are fun, but not just for fun. Each of them can be used as a specific learning tool, and in the ''Comments'' section following each game, we have tried to indicate ways in which they have been successfully used in learning situations.

Before we turn to these learning games themselves, let's consider briefly one game built into the educational system in this country that is a continual source of upset for us — ''The Grading Game.'' A great majority of students, teachers, and administrators take the grading game for granted, and assume that grades are a part of the educational system that always have been present and always must be present. An important step for all of us who are concerned about exploring cooperative, noncompetitive models for learning is to clarify our own values and feelings about grades.

*Playing helps me to see my world in new ways. I would like to extend this by having my students engage in more stimulating simulation games in the classroom.*

Almost all of us are like the fish, who doesn't know what water is until he/she is out of it. We were surrounded by grades when we went to school. What we need is a fresh perspective on grades, what they did to us, and what effect they have on students even now.

It might also be helpful to identify the components of "the grading game." What are the rules? What roles do the players in the game take? What is the objective of the game? Once you have identified the components, you can start making some changes. For example, can you think of ways of changing the goal of "winning at all costs" (get the highest grade you can, no matter what)? One idea might be to eliminate grading on a curve, since this pits one student against another, and often leads to cut-throat practices. How about the rule of "cheat, but don't get caught"? One possibility might be to legitimize "cheating," perhaps by giving tests in which students can collaborate, discuss their answers, share resources, and engage in peer teaching.

Are there ways to change the role of the student in the grading game? The traditional role is to ask one another, after a test is handed back, "wad-ja-get?" How could we help students to ask instead,

"wad-ja-learn?" How can we support students in focusing on the joy of learning, rather than on the joy of "psyching out the teacher?" You'll find answers to these questions (and many more) in an excellent book by Howard Kirschenbaum, Sidney Simon, and Rodney Napier, WAD-JA-GET: THE GRADING GAME IN AMERICAN EDUCATION (New York: Hart, 1971).

Most young people experience competition directly, pervasively, and continuously through playing the grading game. If we can change the grading game, we can impact on students' competitive habits. And if we can do that, we can help them to discover the joys of working and playing together cooperatively. If we are serious about developing learning communities in schools, it is imperative that students *not* see their peers and the teacher as "the enemy," the opposition, the judge and the jury.

Incidentally, lest the idea of "learning games" turn you away with a mumbled "bo-ring," one more thing before we move on to the games. While these are valuable games for classroom use — many of them can be great for a party, too!

Included in this chapter are

quick shuffle

1-2-3-4!

boss, i can't come to work
today

open fist simulation

clay-dough

emotional relay race

human tableaux

picture charades

mutual storytelling

# quick shuffle

Directions to the Players: **Can I have six volunteers to stand up here in a straight line next to me? . . . Great. Now, we'll look at you while you look at us . . . Would you all close your eyes now, while we change our positions up front here . . . Okay, open your eyes and take a look at us now — your job is to put us back together in the same order in which we started out. Each one of you can come up here and shift one of us to a different position in a line, until we're all back together in our original positions. Who wants to begin?**

Comments: QUICK SHUFFLE is a great favorite of many elementary school teachers. It is a perfect companion piece to FIVE CHANGES in the development of perceptual and observational skills.

It is important to structure the reshuffling process as a cooperative group problem-solving technique, rather than allowing one person to be "hero" or "goat" in attempting to place all the players back in their original positions.

# 1-2-3-4!

Directions to the Players: **Would you hop around on either your left foot or your right foot? . . . Now get together with two other people who are hopping around on the same foot you are . . .**

**The three of you stand facing each other, holding one fist clenched in front of you. Shake your fists up and down together four times, and chant together "One, two, three, four!" Those are the only words in this whole game. On the count of four, each of you puts out any number of fingers from zero to five. The object of this game is, without ever talking to each other, for the three of you to have exactly eleven fingers out.**

**Once you've gotten to eleven, try getting to twenty-three with each of you shaking two fists at a time and putting out any number from zero to ten fingers each.**

**Comments:** We are continually amazed at the cries of triumph that issue forth from small groups when the magic eleven fingers appear on their hands. This simple task seems over and over to give people a great sense of achievement, of having accomplished something important. We can't explain it, but it happens time and again.

It is completely up to chance whether it takes your group one try or ten tries to reach the magic number. But in many ways that is one of the unusual beauties of this activity — it is a small-group venture that is completely governed by chance. Unlike many other "team sports" there's no opportunity to be either a heroine or a goat in this one. All the players have an equal input into the group task, and they each have the same opportunity to be the star player . . . none whatsoever!

Teachers and parents of young children will find an additional benefit in playing 1-2-3-4!: it can serve as a lively opportunity for students to practice their addition skills.

# boss, i can't come to work today

Directions to the Players: **Count up the number of letters in your first name, and see if you have an odd number of letters or an even number of letters ... Find a partner who like you has an even or odd number of letters in her or his name ...**

**Notice the sentence on the blackboard, "Boss, I can't come to work today because I've got arthritis, bronchitis, and chronic coughing." We're going to go around the room in order, and you and your partner are going to think of one more word to add on to the end of the sentence. Then one of you can come up and write it on the board and then read back the whole sentence to us. Then it will be the next pair's turn to add a word.**

**Before we proceed, notice that the desciption of the ailments is not a random sequence — there's a reason that each word follows the ones behind it. Anybody see it? ... Sure! The first letters are in alphabetical order: "A" for arthritis, then "B" for bronchitis, "C" for chronic coughing, and so on. And so Michael and Maggie, you can begin and move us right on to the next one.**

**MAGGIE: Boss, I can't come to work today because I've got arthritis, bronchitis, chronic coughing, and diptheria ...**

**Comments:** If you like this game, you'll probably want to read the games in the "Mind Games" chapter as well. In fact, the start of this game can be played like one of the "Guess-My-Rule" games, if you let the players guess the sequence, rather than spelling it out for them. For another good model of that, see SAFARI.

BOSS, I CAN'T COME TO WORK TODAY is useful for increasing vocabulary, memory, and sequencing skills. If your class members are fairly competent in these areas, then it is possible to play this game without the blackboard as a memory aide, and with the participants playing singly, rather than consulting in couples. Pairing, of course, is an effective strategy for making sure that no one will be put "on the spot" without being able to contribute to the group effort.

In a safe way, this game "sanctions" complaining and hypochondria and playing hookey in much the same fun way that HOW TO START AN ARGUMENT sanctions arguing. If you want to bring the experience closer to home, you might title the game DAD, I CAN'T GO TO SCHOOL TODAY (because I've got arthritis . . .). There are a number of variations on this alphabet sequencing technique that you can invent for different purposes. For example, a history review: "One person I certainly admire is Abraham Lincoln: Beard-wearer, Cabin-builder, Debater, Educated at great hardship . . ." Or you might simply want to do a group exercise in sentence construction: "Are boys corruptable? Dorothy (earthy female) gained her insidious joyful kicks making naughty . . ."

Danny Nussbaum invented BOSS, I CAN'T COME TO WORK TODAY for a family car trip. You might like to try it for that, too.

# open fist simulation

Directions to the Players: **Think of your birthday . . . Now join up with one other person so that, when you add your birthdates together (the day of the month), you come up with an** even **number (two** odd **dates or two** even **dates will add up to an even number) . . .**

**I'd like to ask you to do something that is very simple . . . and that is, to make a fist . . . Now, would each of you in the group turn to your partner, and in the next 30 seconds, without any bloodshed or broken bones, see if you can open your partner's fist. You have 30 seconds . . . Go ahead . . . (30 seconds) . . . Time's up!**

**Okay, now that you've had a chance to take on that challenge, I'd like you to do a bit of reflecting on it. Please answer the following three questions to yourself — you may wish to jot a few notes on a piece of paper. (1) From the time that I gave the initial directions (of asking you to make a fist) until when you completed this activity, what were you thinking? — What thoughts went through your mind? . . . (2) What feelings did you experience? — Describe them . . . (3) What did you notice about your own behavior? — What did you do? In other words, I'm asking you to make an inventory of your thoughts, your feelings, and your behaviors. Take a couple minutes to think about this and make some notes to yourself if you like . . .**

**Now that you've each done some private inventorying, I'd like you to turn to your partner again, and take the next few minutes to share your different reflections . . .**

**Okay, now let's take several minutes here in the whole group to sample some of the thoughts, feelings, and behaviors you experienced and observed . . .**

**Comments:** This game can be used simply as a warm-up, to get some energy flowing, to help people get in touch with their neighbors and/or as a learning experience, by adding on the notes, pair-sharing, and group sharing.

This follow-up allows the players to examine the "moral of the story" as they make meaning of their experience. Often they express surprise at how many ways there are to solve one problem . . . or realizing that there are many alternatives to violence (breaking your neighbor's thumb . . . or being pleased that many people share common feelings in this kind of experience.

The qualifying clause in the directions ("without any bloodshed or broken bones") is an important one to add. This is one way of defusing the incredibly ingrained competitive patterns and the "win-at-all-costs" attitudes that are so pervasive.

In essence, this game is a simulation for how people tackle any problem in the world. In this case, the problem is how to open your neighbor's fist. It could just as easily be a metaphor for how to open a student's mind to learning, how to open up communications between countries in the Middle East, or how to tackle the problem of "student discipline." How we tackle the problem of opening our neighbor's fist can give us insight into how we tackle more complex issues.

Thanks to Steven Shakin for sharing the kernel of this activity.

# clay-dough

Directions to the Players: **I'd like each of you to take out something to write with and something to write on. First, draw a circle with two spokes going through it, like this:**

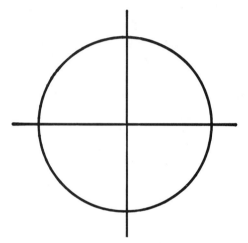

This is a feelings wheel. It's a vehicle that can help you to focus on your feelings . . . How are you feeling right now? At each of the four spokes of the wheel, I'd like you to write down a word that reflects or represents a feeling you are having. Take a couple of minutes to do that just by yourself, without talking with anyone else . . .

Now, flip a coin in your mind . . . If it came up heads, find one other person who's taller than you. If the coin was tails up, find someone shorter than you . . . Get together with your partner and figure out which one of you is "A" and which one is

"B" . . . Okay, let me see the hands of all the A's — there should be one hand going up in each pair. And now let me see the hands of the B's — there should be one hand going up in each apple.

We're going to have an opportunity to do some sculpting now. For the first round, each A will be clay-dough, and each B will be sculptor. A, what you need to do is to pick one of the four words from your feeling wheel, and whisper it in the ear of your partner. B, you then take on the role of sculptor — your task is to "mold" A in the manner of the feeling word he/she just expressed to you. You'll have about one minute to do your sculpting. After that, you'll have a chance to join up with another pair, and engage in some charades for about a minute. They will try to guess your feeling-word sculpting, and vice versa. After that, we'll switch roles, and the B's will have a chance to be clay-dough while the A's take on the sculpting. This will again be followed by the opportunity for you to join with another pair and engage in some mutual guesswork and guessplay.

**Comments:** This is an excellent game to help people ''get in touch'' with themselves (figuratively) and with others (literally). It might be interesting to have people complete a new feelings wheel **after** playing this game. This may reflect the impact that playing can have on how we feel.

In playing this game with younger people, who may not have the verbal/writing skills to complete the feelings wheel, you might choose to have them select pictures from magazines that reflect how they are feeling (putting one picture at each of the four spokes) — or to have them draw their own pictures. Some teachers we know have designed a feelings wheel, in which students can dial-a-feeling at any point during the school day (an excellent means of feedback for the teacher).

Gerry Weinstein invented the wheel (originally called ''the here-and-now wheel'').

# emotional relay race

Directions to the Players: **Find some space for yourself so that you can move around without bumping into anyone else. Take a couple of minutes to come up with your own sound-and-movement that can be easily repeated by you and that expresses the feeling of ''happiness''** ...
Remember your sound-and-movement for happiness, and now come up with one for ''sadness'' ... And now make up one for ''anger,'' an angry sound-and-movement that you could repeat exactly, over and over if you had to ...

You'll notice on the floor over there one bowl with an apple, one with a pear, and one with a banana. Decide which one of those you would rather eat and line up behind it ...

We're going to do a relay race right now with three teams: the Apples, the Bananas, and the Pears. The first person in line picks up your team's piece of fruit and runs over to those bowls over there. Put your fruit into the bowl in your lane, do your angry sound-and-movement three complete times, and then run back to the starting bowl. Do your happy sound-and-movement twice. Run back to the red bowl and do your sad sound-and-movement three times. Then pick up your piece of fruit, run back to the start, take a bite out of the fruit, and then hand it to the next person in line, who begins the same race over again ...

**Comments:** In general we are not fond of relay races, because there seems to be no way to take the competition out of them. It is difficult for the players to take EMOTIONAL RELAY RACE competitively, however, because of its zany race requirements (most of the "contestants" spend more time shrieking with laughter than they do running) and because of the completely arbitrary way the teams are set up.

Of course, one team *will* finish first in the race (especially if there are five players on the Apple team and twelve on the Bananas and on the Pears, for example), but one easy way to remedy that is to have all of the players run through the course three times, shuttling between the various teams.

EMOTIONAL RELAY RACE is an excellent classroom activity for introducing students to the value of the public expression of inner feelings. It can deal with some "heavy" feelings, but in a lighthearted, non-threatening mode of expression.

Players generally have an easier time creating their sound-and-motions if they have first played HOW TO START AN ARGUMENT, CRESCENDO and REBOUND (see Chapters 3 and 5).

# human tableaux

Directions to the Players: **Get together in a group of (three, four or five)[1] people, and find out the names of the people in your group . . . Take a few minutes by yourself to think of a time when you were very happy. Think about an actual event from your life — what happened, who was there, where it took place, what you all looked like**

One at a time, in our groups we're each going to take a turn making tableaux — pictures frozen in time — about our experiences being happy. You are not going to be an actress or an actor in your own tableaux — you're going to be the director. The first thing to do is to share with your group the story of what happened to you that time you were happy.

Then pick one person to play you, and one person to play each of the other people involved in your story, and set them up in a frozen moment in time when the story is at its height.

You can direct your group members to show a certain emotion on their face, to hold their bodies in a certain way, and to be in a certain position in relation to each other, just the way it was for you in real life. Remember, there is no action here, and no talking — just a frozen picture. And when it's all set up to the director's satisfaction, then we'll move on to the next director, until all five people in your group have had a chance to set up their tableaux. Then we'll all show our tableaux to the whole group.

**Comments:** It is generally helpful if the group leader sets up a demonstration tableaux of an incident from her own life as an example of the process.

The tableaux does not have to be restricted to the emotion of happiness, of course. Sad, powerless, surprised, excited, jealous, angry, and many other emotional memories all can lead to effective tableaux.

Legitimizing a student's emotional experiences is an important and an often-neglected component of education. HUMAN TABLEAUX, CLAY-DOUGH, and EMOTIONAL RELAY RACE are three activities that are helpful in allowing students to begin to share with each other their present feelings and their emotional past. All three activities allow the sharing of emotional material in a safe, creative, and non-judgmental manner.

We first learned about HUMAN TABLEAUX from Carol Korty when she was directing the UMass Children's Theatre Ensemble.

---

[1]The playleader will need to decide in advance which size small group will evenly divide the larger group.

# picture charades

Directions to the Players: **How many of you can draw? . . . My guess is that many of you, upon hearing that question, had ''vultures'' flocking around in your mind, telling you ''of course, you can't draw . . . remember your second grade teacher told you that the sun should be in the upper right hand corner, and not the upper left hand corner! Many of us carry around these vulture phrases about our drawing, our singing, and many other activities in life. I'd like to prove to you in this game that you** *can* **draw — and your drawings can communicate ideas to the other players.**

**How many of you have played the game, ''charades''? . . . The way that game is usually played is that people use their bodies to act out or represent the word or phrase to be discovered. For our purposes, in this game, we will be using drawing to help uncover or discover the charades words. It follows that the name of this game is PICTURE CHARADES!! Everyone will need a pencil and paper . . .**

**To start off, everyone will need to do a quick draw. That is, I'd like you each to take a piece of paper and draw a clock with the hands anywhere you want them. The next step is for you literally to take some steps . . . I'd like you to form groups of four by joining up with three other people whose clocks show** *different* **times from your own . . .**

**Now that you're in quads, I'd like the members in each group to count off 1-2-3-4. We'll start the game by having #1 in each group come up to me. I will whisper a sweet something into each #1's ear. That sweet something will be a word that the #1 will then take back to his/her group. Your task, #1, is to draw/illustrate/represent the word in such a way that your three partners could guess what it is. Once they have guessed it, #2 comes up to me to receive the next word to be illustrated.**

**There's a safety valve built into this game: if two of your three partners who are trying to guess the word want to give up and go on to a new word, those two people just have to call out ''aunt.'' When two people in your quartet ''cry aunt,'' person #1 will tell the word. Then, person #2 in your group will come up to me, and I will whisper another sweet something into #2's ear. #2 will then return to his/her quad, and illustrate the new word, which your partners will try to guess.**

**We'll keep recycling for about 10-15 minutes. If all four people in your group have had a chance to draw, then have #1 come up to me for ''seconds.'' Any questions on the directions? . . . Okay #1's, come on up and let me whisper in your ear . . .**

**Comments:** It is usually best for the leader to start off by giving some ''easy,'' concrete words for the first couple of artists in each group. For instance, the word ''cow'' or the word ''moon'' would probably be easier to represent/guess than a more abstract word like ''happiness.'' This helps to get the momentum going and growing.

Once a group begins to recycle, that is, when #1 comes up for a second time, we like to give the players more responsibility for the direction and content of the game. This can be done easily by whispering to #1 the second time around ''pick your own word, and illustrate it.''

What usually happens is that the concentration in each group is intense. When there are many groups working simultaneously, it is difficult to keep track of who is ''ahead'' — anyway, there will be no awards to the group that has worked on eighty-three words, as opposed to the group that has worked on three words. The beauty of this game is that it is flexibly structured, so that each group can work at its own pace. It is important that the players understand that it is no disgrace to have their teammates ''cry aunt.'' Make a special effort to detoxify this potentially-competitive part of PICTURE CHARADES.

The purpose of this game is to make connections between the illustrator and the guessers. By having the drawer and the guessers on the same team, the sense of cooperation and connectedness is heightened. A fringe benefit of this game often appears in the form of increased awareness and appreciation for the creativity of group members. There are usually as many ways to draw a particular word as there are people in the room. It's often interesting afterwards to see how different players illustrated the same words. This helps everyone to see that, in fact, there is no ''right answer'' when it comes to creativity, and that it is important for us to respect (and celebrate) individual differences!

# mutual storytelling

Directions to the Players: **With the popularity of the novel** *Roots,* **people are becoming more interested in the idea of oral history. We're going to do a game together that's based on some actual storytelling techniques in other cultures. In our little community here, let's assume that there are some basic stories that we all know, that the storyteller tells over and over again.**

**However, so it won't get boring, we've invented a technique so that** *anyone* **can take over the story and change it at any time. The way to do that is to interrupt the story and say "I was present!" Well, if you were** *present,* **obviously you know more than the storyteller. So I would say to you, "What did you see, my friend?" And you would add whatever details you wanted to add to the story, and take it in whatever direction you felt like. And when you are finished, we'll all say "Aha!" So let's all try that together: ("AHA!")**

**Then the storyteller will continue with the story, being sure to continue right where you left off. The only guideline is that you can't deny something that someone else has witnessed. If someone was present and saw our hero jump off a cliff, you can't say: "I was present . . . he didn't really jump off a cliff." Yes, he did jump off that cliff — you have to take it from there. And don't worry about making**
the most brilliant contribution anybody has ever thought of for the story — just say the first thing that comes into your head. Because *anything* that moves our story along is going to be brilliant.**

**Okay, who has a story we all know that we can make up our own version of. ("Little Red Riding Hood!") All right. Once upon a time there was a young woman named Little Red Riding Hood, and her parents gave her a big basket of goodies to take to her grandmother's house. This was a very heavy basket of goodies she had — show me the way Red Riding Hood could barely lift this basket, and show me the way she finally got it up onto her shoulder, and leaning to one side, began staggering through the woods (players all stagger through the woods) . . . ("I was present!") And what did you see my friend? ("I saw her put her basket down and take out an apple, and decide to hitchhike through the woods, instead!") (AHA!) That was very observant of you, my friend. Yes, indeed — show me the way Red Riding Hood was munching on her apple and stuck out her thumb and tried to flag down a passing Volkswagen as it drove by . . . Was anyone present to see who was driving that Volkswagen? . . .**

**Comments:** Obviously the story can take off in a million and one madcap directions from here. It is important for the storyteller to keep the players "physicalizing" the story (doing the actions, becoming the avalanche, making the crying noises) or the game will degenerate into pure talk. Once in a while the players will become so enamored of the physicalization that they will use it to wonderful effect. For instance, once a participant said, ("I was present! And so Hansel and Gretel jumped on each other's backs and ran around the house!") and the effect was instantly-energizing as all the players scrambled to piggy-back on top of each other!!

In the classroom MUTUAL STORYTELLING can be used as a creativity exercise, with the participants constructing a group fantasy together out of whole cloth. This exercise can be made more content-oriented, allowing the class members, for example, to have a bit of fun with their history assignments. Using the MUTUAL STORYTELLING structure, class members can devise their own versions of historical reality, based on events that actually happened — "Let's hear the *real* story of Grant and Lee at Appomattox!"

This story-telling game is based loosely on the work of Mara Capy. Mara does audience-participation storytelling concerts, based on traditional African folk tales.

Laughing and learning are not mutually exclusive. In fact, many studies indicate that playfulness and enjoyment free up people's attention, so that retention increases. By learning to play cooperatively, people can be more playful and effective in their learning. The games in this chapter outline ways students (and other learners) can combine education and entertainment. If Mark Twain had been given a chance to play these games in school, he probably would have noted that his schooling enhanced — rather than interfered with — his education!

# 8 mind games,
## or why is a half-defrosted steak

Because neither one is very well thawed out!

Here are some involving games to help stretch the ol' grey matter upstairs. These games are excellent ways to help players think creatively, see the world through new and different glasses, and do some cooperative problem solving. [1]

The Mind Games in this chapter can be used in coordination with games from a number of other chapters. The first thing you need to know is that these are great games for livening up a dead party! Games like CAHOOTS, RASPUTIN, and SAFARI can provide partygoers with hours of creative interaction. These games, plus activities like the MIND-STRETCHERS, can also be effective games for classroom learning if they are used to expand the learners' problem-solving and logical-thinking faculties. And in

conjunction with some of the other games in the ''Intimate and Family Games'' chapter, a game like NAME CIRCLES can turn a long family car trip into a pleasure cruise.

One word of caution: be careful in using these games. If they are improperly handled there is a chance that the players will feel ''stupid'' when they come up against a real puzzler. For that reason it is especially important to read the ''Comments'' following each game, which are designed to assist you in maximizing the *nourishing* nature of these games and minimizing the potentially toxic aspects.

Games we have included for your journey into expanded thinking include

**safari**
**mind reading**
   (**cahoots and rasputin**)
**name circles**
**either-or metaphors**
**mind-stretchers**

[1] Joel Goodman and Irv Furman's MAGIC AND THE EDUCATED RABBIT provides hundreds of additional ideas, magic tricks, and riddles which you can use as brainteasers and as tools for teaching/learning. This book is available through Sagamore Institute, 110 Spring St., Saratoga Springs, NY 12866.

# like an impulsive idea?

# safari

Directions to the Players: **SAFARI is the most open-ended of a group of games that are known as "guess-my-rule games." It is possible to create endless variations of SAFARI.**

**The best known of the guess-my-rule games is "Fanny Dooley." Fanny Dooley loves walls but hates ceilings; loves carriages but hates babies; loves dental floss and toothpaste but hates brushing; loves cigarettes and hates cigars; loves streets and alleys, but hates highways and parkways.**

**As in all of these games, the objective is to guess the rule that determines what Fanny Dooley loves and what she hates, by offering examples. Does she love potatoes? "No, she hates potatoes, but she loves peppers" . . . That goes on until we guess the rule, which in this case is that Fanny Dooley loves everything that has a double letter in it, and hates everything that does not.**

**In SAFARI, one person announces that s/he is going on a safari, and tells what s/he will bring along. The rest of us work as a team to guess the rule by going around in order and offering things that we can bring along. The person originating the safari responds to each item, saying whether or not we can bring it on the safari (that is, whether or not it conforms to the rule to be guessed by the group). Between**

guesses, group members try to help each other figure out the underlying rule for the safari. For example:

**BILL: I'm going on a safari and I'm going to bring my dog, and a bridge table. Who wants to come along?**

**SUZETTE: I do. Can I bring a book?**

**BILL: No.**

(GROUP DISCUSSION: Maybe it has to do with the fact that both "dog" and "bridge table" have the letter "D" in them. Let's test that one out.)

**PEGGY: Can I bring my doorknob?**

**BILL: No.**

(GROUP DISCUSSION: Okay, forget the "D" theory. Who's next?)

**ERIC: Can I bring a cat?**

**BILL: Yes.**

(GROUP DISCUSSION: Allright! Maybe it has something to do with animals. But where does the bridge table fit in? Let's try another animal.)

VIC: Can I bring a snake?

BILL: No.

(GROUP DISCUSSION: There's more to it than just animals. Maybe it's animals that normally live indoors or something. Whose turn it it?)

SUZETTE: Mine. Can I bring a spider?

BILL: No.

(GROUP DISCUSSION: Nope, not indoor animals. Let's try something to do with the bridge table.)

PEGGY: Can I bring a pool table?

BILL: Yes.

(GROUP DISCUSSION: Okay, a bridge table and a pool table. It probably has something to do with tables that you play games on. Let's try another.)

ERIC: Can I bring a ping-pong table?

BILL: No.

(GROUP DISCUSSION: Well, that's not it. Maybe it has something to do with playing, though . . . )

VIC: Can I bring a ping-pong paddle?

BILL: No.

(GROUP DISCUSSION: It doesn't look like it has to do with play. Let's see what we've got so far. Two kinds of tables, and a cat and a dog. Maybe it has to do with sitting — you know, the way the animals can "sit" and the way you sit at a table . . . )

SUZETTE: Okay, can I bring a chair?

BILL: What kind of a chair?

SUZETTE: My desk chair.

BILL: Yes.

(GROUP DISCUSSION: Hunh. Anybody got any theories? Doesn't look as if our spider question really solved that indoor-outdoor thing — some spiders can live indoors and outdoors. Let's try that one again.)

ERIC: Can I bring an elephant?

BILL: Yes.

(GROUP DISCUSSION: It must definitely have something to do with animals. How about animals that can sit at a table, you know, the way the elephants do in the circus ... )

And so we keep on going, sharing with each other our hunches about what the underlying rule might be, until our group has figured out the rule, which in this case is that we can only bring things with four legs on the safari.

Okay, I'm going on a safari and I'm going to bring something wonderful, and a toothpick, and the Threepenny Opera, and some fortified vitamins. Who wants to come along? ...

Comments: The secret of successful guessing in SAFARI is not in being ''smarter'' than other people, but in working together to look at things in a way that is different than usual: in noticing that everything on the safari has a hidden number in it (like *won*derful, *too*thpick, etc.) or has something to do with the color red, or has the letter ''o'' followed by two

consonants, or whatever crazy rule someone has cooked up.

Because many of us are not used to thinking in this way, SAFARI can become a very frustrating experience. Most of us have been told in one way or another, that we are "stupid" (or not as smart as the next person, anyway) and because of that, all these mental games can begin to bring up feelings of anxiety in the players, especially if there is any hint of a competition for who is going to get the "right" answer first — or that "everybody else has it figured out already except for me! They all must be laughing at me!"

To keep a safari from moving in this toxic direction it is imperative that all the players work together as a team, continually sharing their hunches about the rule with each other. Encourage such cooperative efforts, and actively discourage individual players from calling out guesses randomly, trying to be the first one to get the "right" answer.

Every guess made by a member of the group is helpful in supplying data about the solution, of course. We are continually building on each other's ideas and suggestions as we move towards the final solution to the problem. So we are always working together as a group, and openly acknowledging that fact will minimize any pressure to "perform," and will also prevent feelings of "I'm stupid" among the group members. People who are inventing safaris should be reminded, too, that the object of a safari is to stretch the group's (collective) brain — not to "stump" them or to "beat" them! SAFARI is a "game" in the sense that it is a playful exercise — it is not a contest with winners and losers!

A favorite SAFARI in elementary schools is "Picnic." "We're going on a picnic and Joel is going to bring some jam, and Matt is going to bring some mushrooms. Wanna come?" "What can we bring?" (The hidden rule of this picnic is that you have to bring something that starts with the same letter as your own first name . . . )

The joy of guess-my-rule games comes in making that mental leap that ties together (apparently) disparate items. After the rule has been guessed by the group, it's often helpful to go around and give each person a chance to think of one thing they would bring along that conforms to the rule that has now been discovered.

We learned about SAFARI from the masters of the art, Bernie DeKoven and Rocky DeKoven, at The Games Preserve in Fleetwood, Pennsylvania.

# mind reading

Directions to the Players: **Mind reading games are really disguised Guess-my-rule games in which the two mind-readers pretend to be displaying mental telepathy, but everyone knows that they have really concocted an elaborate system for passing information back and forth secretly. So the game becomes "guess-my-code." Two of the best examples of mind-reading games are CAHOOTS and RASPUTIN. Here's how they go:**

## rasputin

Matt: Joel will go out of the room for a minute, and someone here will tell me the name of a famous person that we all know, and I will communicate that person's name to Joel by the famous system of Russian mental telepathy. Who has a name? (Muhammed Ali) .... **Come on back in, Joel .... (Claps three times) ... Rasputin ... (Clap) ... Mendeleyev Rasputin ... Tchaikovsky Hruschev ... (Clap-Clap) ...Rasputin ... Gorky Raskolnikov ... (Clap-Clap) (Clap) ... Tchigorin ... (Clap-Clap) ... Shastikovitch Turgenev Rasputin.**

Joel: Muhammed Ali.

(The other players begin tearing their hair out and jumping up and down screaming in disbelief ....)

## cahoots

JOEL: I'm going to put this pillow case over Matt's head so he can't see anything, and then we as a group are going to silently pick out one of us. I'm going to point to a number of people, and when I come to the person we've picked out, Matt is going to tell me who it is. (The group picks someone). Are you in Cahoots?

MATT: Yes.

JOEL: Do you point as I point? (Pointing to someone)

MATT: Yes.

JOEL: Do you point as I point?

MATT: Yes.

JOEL: Do you point as I point?

MATT: Yes.

JOEL: To whom do I point?

MATT: Nancy!

(Gasps of astonishment and "Do it again!" from the other players).

**Comments:** Mind reading games can be **much** more frustrating than even guess-my-rule games and we strongly suggest that the players who are guessing work together as a team and pool their information. One person guessing alone and trying to figure out RASPUTIN can be driven to the brink! In many cases it is advisable to have the mind readers answer yes-or-no questions from the other players as they go along. ("Does it have anything to do with your tone of voice? With your body position? Is the order in which you point to the people important? Does Rasputin mean something special?") Once you get the hang of CAHOOTS and RASPUTIN, you can devise your own coded systems. If you want the "Secrets" revealed, read on.

**RASPUTIN:** Bernie DeKoven tried out RASPUTIN on Matt and Pamela Kekich and drove them crazy one night trying to figure it out. In the example above, Joel and Matt are obviously spelling out something, but it's clear that they're not spelling out "Muhammed Ali." The first thing we notice is that "Rasputin" appears all over the place, and is also the name of the game — so it must mean something special. And it does: it means "end of the word." Obviously the claps mean something too. But what? Let's write out

the first letter of each word of the message, leaving out the claps and the Rasputins. We get: ____M TH__ GR____ T__ST. A strange message! One thing we notice about it is that it's all consonants — where are the vowels? Aha! The claps must be the vowels! AEIOU. One Clap for A, two for E, three for I, four for O, five for U. Okay, let's fill in the vowels and take another look at it: I AM THE GREATEST. Fabulous! It must be Muhammed Ali! What is spelled out in RASPUTIN is not the name of the person under consideration but the clue about that person's identity. So the game never gets boring for the two mindreaders — their own creativity gets pushed to its limits in the clues they think up. There are many different ways to give clues for Muhammed Ali, and no two people will do it the same. You could try "Float Like A Butterfly, Sting Like A Bee," "Ex-Heavy Weight Champ," "Rope-A-Dope" or many others. So it helps to know something about your partner and his or her field of expertise!

In reading over the coded message, one thing still might look strange: "Hruschev". And you thought his name was spelled "Khruschev!" didn't you? Well, you'll find out you're not going to come up with any famous Russian names for certain letters — try "H" and "W" off the top of your head — so you'll have to set up certain fixed code words in advance for those letters. ''Hruschev'' and ''Wintrograd'' are our old favorites.

The world's quickest clue: Vassily Rasputin (for Winston Churchill or Thomas Pynchon).

The world's funniest clue (Bernie DeKoven's brainstorm): Fyodor Raskolnikov (Clap-Clap) Nijinsky Checkov Hruschev Rasputin ... Nureyev (Clap Clap-Clap-Clap) Vladivostok (Clap-Clap) Lermontov (Clap-Clap-Clap) Stalin Tchaikovsky Rasputin ... Spassky Checkov Raskolnikov (Clap-Clap-Clap-Clap) Tchigorin (Clap-Clap-Clap-Clap-Clap) Minsk Rasputin. (Answer: Balzac)

**CAHOOTS:** The beauty of CAHOOTS lies in its simplicity. In fact, it is so simple that uninitiated players always concoct theories that are much too complicated in an attempt to unravel it. The obvious thing that everyone seizes upon is that the ''message'' is being communicated by the pointer, and that some complicated sequence is at work (''Let's see, I was the third person he pointed to, and then Dave, and then Sylvia; then the next time he pointed to Sylvia first, so...'') In fact, however, in the example above, Matt knew that Nancy was the one who had been chosen before any of the pointing started! The key to the code is the question ''Are you in Cahoots?'' Freely translated, that question means ''The person who just spoke (even if it was to say something like ''when are you going to get started?'') is the person the group has picked. Did you recognize their voice?'' If Matt did recognize the voice, he says ''Yes'' and we proceed as in the example above. If he isn't clear, he answers ''No'' to the question of ''Are you in Cahoots?'', and then Joel tries to get Nancy to speak again (perhaps with an innocent question like ''This one may take a little time: is that all right with everybody?''; as soon as Nancy says ''yes'', Joel quickly asks Matt ''Are you in Cahoots?'' As in the guess-my-rule games, the key to deciphering CAHOOTS is to approach it with no preconceptions, back away from what *seems* to be happening, and all of a sudden everything becomes clear.

# name circles

Directions to the Players: **Let's all form a circle! We're going to take turns going around the circle, with each person free-associating the name of a well-known person, based loosely on the name that came before it. So, for example, if the person before you gave ''Bruce Springsteen,'' you might say ''Albert Einstein,'' making a link between the sound of these two last names. Or you might offer ''Bruce Dern,'' linking up the two first names. Or you might say ''Somerset Maugham.'' Now that's a little trickier, but it's perfectly acceptable — this time the link is in the subject, not the sound: ''summer'' and ''spring''. The object of the game is for us as a group to bring the string of associations back full circle, so we've gotten back to the original name — in this case, back to ''Bruce Springsteen.'' Here's a short example with Joel's name: Joel Goodman, Noel, Santa Claus, Good Samaritan, Joel Goodman.**

**Comments:** If a person gets ''stuck'', s/he can ''pass''. The object of the game is to keep the associations moving, and *not* to embarrass any of the individual players. Here are more examples using Matt's and Joel's names:

1. Matt Weinstein, Bruce Springsteen, Paul Winter, Paolo Freire, Frere Jacques, Jack Dempsey, C.C. Rider, Dee Dee Sharp, e.e. cummings, Bob Cummings, Bobby Wine, Matt Weinstein.

2. Matt Weinstein, Matt Helm, Hellman's Mayonnaise, Doctor Mayo, E.L. Doctorow, Rowan and Martin, Martin van Buren, Van Johnson, Lyndon Johnson, Lucky Lindy, Lucky Luciano, Lucille Ball, Belle of the Ball, Bella Lugosi, Bella Abzug, Abner Doubleday, Tuesday Weld, Rick Monday, Ricky Nelson, Admiral Nelson, Harry Neilson, Neil Simon, Carly Simon, Empress Carlotta, Lotte Lenya, Lenny Bruce, Bruce Springsteen, Matt Weinstein.

3. Joel Goodman, Benny Goodman, Ben Gay, Gaylord Perry, Lord of the Flies, William Golding, Good Will, Joel Goodman.

A cousin of NAME CIRCLES is HINK PINK. In this game, a player thinks of a combination of two rhyming words, having the same number of syllables. S/he then gives a descriptive clue, from which the other players try to guess the two-word combination. The originator says ''hink pink'' if each of the words has one syllable, ''hinky pinky'' if each of the words has two syllables, and so forth ...

hink pink: a fishbowl for my hotdogs

(a frank tank)

Hinky pinky: the place where I sent my hotdogs out to be washed and pressed.

(a weiner cleaner)

# either-or metaphors

Directions to the Players: **The name of this game is EITHER-OR METAPHORS. In order to play it, what we'll need to do first is form groups of two. I'd like to ask each of you individually now to make a choice: Are you an "either" or are you an "or"? Once you've figured out who you are, then mill around and find your partner: each "either" will look for another "either" and each "or" will look for another "or" to join up with (or an "oar", if you want to create a row)...**

**Now that you've "meta" your partner, I'd like you to focus on some metaphorical choices. There are no "correct" answers! Here's the first one: "which of these travels faster — a lead weight dropped off a cliff, or a rumor?" Take some time now with your partner to talk about your choices, and how you arrived at your decisions. Remember, we're not "scoring" these answers, we just want to see where everybody goes with this! ...**

**Okay, let's sample a couple of responses now in the whole group. Who chose "lead weight?" What were some of your reasons? ... And now can we have some people speak for "rumor"? ... What made you choose that one? ...**

**Ready for Round Two? "Which of these takes up more room: a hippopotamus, or a laugh?" Again, with your partner, take a few minutes to explore this choice and the**

different ways of looking at it . . .

**Okay, let's hear it in the group. Can we have some hippo-supporters share their thinking on how they arrived at their choice? ... and now, how about some laugh-leaners ... what led you to your choice? ...**

**There's an old Chinese proverb that goes something like this: "I hear and forget; I see and I remember; I do and I understand." In line with this proverb, I'd like to provide you with an opportunity to do, as a way of increasing your understanding — and as a way of making this game more memorable. So, without any further a-do, how about if we have all the hippo-choosers joining together, and forming one huge hippo en masse. See how much room you can take up ... go to it, hippos! ...**

**And now, laughers, it's your turn. See how much of the room you can fill up with your laughter. On your mark, get set, ho (ho ho).**

**Comments:** Metaphors are an excellent medium for helping people to stretch their imagination muscles. When players have to compare apples and oranges, lead weights and rumors, laughs and hippos, it requires a great deal of mind-stretching. The creative perceptions and interpretations which emerge during the pair- and whole-group discussions can be hilarious, insightful, . . . and sometimes awe-full!

Of course, there are an infinite number of these either-or choices which you could present . . . Or, better yet, that your players, can invent. Why not give them an opportunity, after you've presented a couple of choices, to generate some either-ors of their own, which they, in turn, could present to the other players?

You might find yourself playing with such ticklers as: "which is more dangerous: a hungry mosquito or a constipated hippo?" The acting out, the doing, of this question, can be a real gasser.

Of course, the very basic guideline to this kind of game is that there is no "right answer." Be sure to free the players' thinking, by letting them know beforehand that they won't be "marked down" for choosing "lead weight," nor will they be wrong if they choose "rumor." The object is to encourage divergent thinking, to invite unusual associations, rather than to converge on the "right answer." This is important to keep in mind, especially in cases where 90% of the group chooses "lead weight" and only 10% chooses "rumor". It would be a terrible rumor to suggest that majority rules in a game like this (drop it like a lead weight!).

William Gordon (President, Synectics Education Systems, 121 Brattle Street, Cambridge, MA 02138) can provide you with dozens of publications that creatively play around with metaphorical ways of learning.

An enjoyable off-shoot, and a way of personalizing this game even more, is to have the players focus on *self*-metaphors. For instance, you could ask them to make the following kinds of either-or choices . . . are you

(1) more like a bing, a bang, or a boing?
(2) more like a backbone, a funnybone, a hambone, a jawbone, or a trombone?
(3) more like a calm lake, a bubbling brook, a flood, or a swamp?
(4) more like New York City, Cheyenne, or Paris?
(5) more like _____ or _____ (you fill in the blanks).

# mind-stretchers

Directions to the Players: **Do you mind if I joke? . . . Now you may be wondering just what I have in mind by that statement. Actually, it's just a way of introducing a game called MIND-STRETCHERS.**

**We're all probably familiar with the ol' brain teasers, puzzles on which we wrack our brains for hours and hours, if not days and days on end, trying to figure out. I'll be presenting you with a series of mind-stretchers. Instead of being on your own, in isolation, trying to solve them, I'd like to invite you, if you choose, to join up with as many as three other people to be your collaborating detectives. What you need to do first is to make a choice: "do I want to work/play alone, do I want to join up with one other person, do I want to hook up with two others, or do I want to be with three other detectives in trying to figure out the mind-stretchers?" Okay, at the end of the next minute, I'd like you to have decided with whom, if anyone, you'd like to work . . .**

**I'll be posting on the board twenty-four mind-stretchers. Each one of these stands for a familiar word or phrase that we've all heard at one time or another. Work at your own pace, and in your own space. We'll check back with each other in a little while, compare ideas, and look for the "answers in the back of the book."**

**Comments:** It is vital to give people a choice as to whether they want to work alone or with others. Some players will enjoy working alone, challenging themselves to decode the puzzles, while others will find more support in playing with other detectives. Presenting this game in such a way that there is flexibility to accommodate both styles is what gives the players themselves more control over the game.

At the end, after re-viewing different ways of viewing each puzzle, it's often intriguing to challenge the players to generate some additional mind-stretchers themselves, which they could then present to others. In essence, this would allow for the game to be self-renewing ad-infinitum.

As with other puzzle games, it is crucial to be sensitive to frustration levels. Too many of us already have vultures which occupy space "upstairs," get in the way of us figuring out puzzles, and swoop down on us when we don't figure 'em out. It might even be helpful to explicitly state that to the group before starting.

This game is an excellent one for stretching our creativity muscles and our learning muscles. The process of decoding is the same as the process of making the strange familiar . . . *learning*. The process of coding (creating your own puzzles) is the same as the process of making the familiar strange . . . *creating*.

| | | | |
|---|---|---|---|
| EZ<br>‾‾‾‾<br>iiiii | TOUCH *(written vertically)* | MOTH<br>CRY<br>CRY<br>CRY | BLACK<br>——<br>COAT |
| TIME<br>TIME | S A N D *(written diagonally)* | HURRY ↗ | ME QUIT |
| LE<br>VEL | KNEE<br>——<br>LIGHT | MAN<br>——<br>OVER | HE'S / HIMSELF |
| R\|E\|A\|D\|I\|N\|G | **AGES** | R<br>R O A D<br>A<br>D | Ø<br>——<br>M.D.<br>PH.D.<br>L.L.D. |
| WEAR<br>——<br>LONG | DICE<br>DICE | ECNALG | CYCLE<br>CYCLE<br>CYCLE |
| CHAIR | TOWN *(written vertically)* | ii   ii<br>O    O | STAND<br>——<br>I |

Answers to MIND-STRETCHERS:

1. easy on the eyes
2. touchdown
3. mothballs
4. black overcoat
5. double time
6. shifting sand
7. hurry up
8. quit following me
9. split level
10. neon light
11. man overboard!
12. he's beside himself
13. reading between the lines
14. dark ages
15. crossroads
16. 3 degrees below zero (a weather report)
17. long underwear
18. paradise
19. glance backwards
20. tricycle
21. high chair
22. downtown
23. circles under the eyes
24. I understand

Dot Michener first showed us these MIND STRETCHERS.

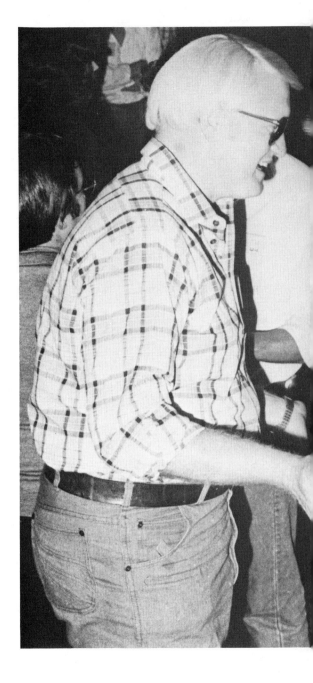

What is the quietest sport? . . . .
Bowling, because you can hear a pin drop!
This chapter has included a number of
riddles and mind-stretching activities that
require two skills simultaneously: (1)
intra-personal: critical thinking; (2)
inter-personal: cooperating. These
activities demonstrate that by working
together, tackling challenges can be fun!
We invite you to generate additional mind
games to get your own wheels turning and
to build a spirit of cooperation in your
group.

# 9 games for leadership and organizational

The games in this chapter can be used as tools for promoting group leadership skills and for organizational development. Therapists, group-leaders, and management consultants who have trained with us have had successful experiences using these ''soft'' playful techniques in working with their clients. We believe that a fun approach to working with groups can also be a serious one, and this chapter shares some of the ways in which playful group experiences can be used to generate some more ''serious'' results.

# training
# development

*Let's bring back Peter Pan ... Play
has an age-less quality about it.
Playing is a mature activity for adults.*

Games like THREE POSITIONS and
FIVE CHANGES, both described in this
chapter, can be used both as light-hearted
icebreakers at a party, and as vehicles for
self-examination of individual leadership
styles in a training session. The game itself
need not be changed, simply the questions
that are asked following the game by the
play facilitator. A sensitive organizational
development trainer can follow up the
games with a series of questions designed
to illuminate the players' behavior, on a
level that might not be readily apparent to
people who think they are "just playing a
game." "Did you pick a man or a woman
as a partner? Did you pick someone you
know well, or someone you don't know at
all? How did your team develop its
strategy? What part did you take in
leadership and team decision-making? Is

that typical of your behavior?" Such
questions can allow the players to see their
participation in the game as a reflection of
their attitudes/behavior in other settings
— at work, for example. The "Comments"
following some of the games in this chapter
suggest questions that might be
appropriate for this type of learning. Such
a learning process is a powerful
experience, and should be carefully
facilitated by a qualified trainer. It is NOT
recommended as a casual exercise to be led
by persons — including managers — who
have a vested interest in the outcomes.

One of the most exhilarating experiences
a player can have is to take leadership in a
group. Many people handle it easily, while
many others have a really hard time. A
number of the games in this chapter have
been designed to give the players an
experience of leading the group for a time,
and then passing the leadership on to
another player (See STOP AND GO,
TOUCH BLUE, ELBOW FRUIT HOP, THE
CARGO CULT). A qualified and sensitive

trainer working with these games can diagnose each player's readiness to take leadership in the group. By careful post-game discussion with the players the trainer can help them to gain insight into their individual decision-making and leadership styles.

*Being unique and feeling unique is vital to me. I need to be uniquely me when I play. I enjoy "making up my own rules" — changing the game to fit the situation.*

The familiar models of facilitated group play have one principal group "leader," who takes the players through the entire experience. A "parent-child" dependence can begin to develop between such a leader and group. The "shared leadership" games in this chapter offer an alternative model. While the leader sets up the basic rules of the game, s/he then fades into the background and becomes an *equal* player. Responsibility for the game flowing and evolving then belongs to the whole group. When the game works, everyone can share in the glory!

Of course, an important component of any organizational program is the development of a sense of community among the members of the group. We like to point to the family as a model for community: members can argue with each other, can even scream and shout and carry on — but at base they are committed to loving each other and being with each other and supporting each other. My father and I may have an argument at breakfast, but that doesn't mean that we will refuse to ever have another meal together. Underlying all our family disagreements is mutual love, respect and commitment to "working things out." All of the cooperative games and exercises in this book can contribute to the construction of a similar (if less intense) "family" atmosphere in any task-group or organization.

A trainer and group leader who is concerned with building a sense of support and community should be aware that even the way in which you divide the players into groups can be counterproductive to the building of a supportive environment. Recall "A Note on Choosing Partners and Forming Groups" in Chapter 2. You can think of as many non-threatening ways to get people into groups as to get them into pairs. ANIMALS, BIRTHDAYS, CHORALE OF THE VOWELS, and INCORPORATIONS will also give you ideas.

*Play could be . . . power, group approval, friendship, bright atmosphere, being needed, love acceptance, excitement, adventure, challenge, group creativity, teamwork, personal satisfaction, a way of changing society.*

The games we have chosen for this chapter all offer joyful, non-threatening opportunities for team building and leadership assessment. Try some of these with your group:

**three positions**
**five changes**
**stop and go**
**touch blue**
**elbow fruit hop**
**the cargo cult**

# three positions

Directions to the Players: **Would you rather be eating a plum, a peach, or a strawberry? . . . Get together in a group with everyone here who has picked the same fruit you have . . . Stand in a line with the other people in your group so you can see everyone else — so the three teams will be lined up in a big triangle . . .**

This game is called THREE POSITIONS. Let's start with our hands at our sides, standing up straight — that will be our "neutral position." Any variation on that we're going to call a "position" — it can be a gross variation or a subtle one. So who can show us our first variation? . . . Okay, let's all do what Laura is doing, hands over head, that'll be our first position . . . Back to neutral. Who has a second position for us, different from the first? . . . Okay, let's all try that one, squatting down . . . Now let's try position number one again . . . Good — now back to neutral. Will someone show us a third and final position, different from the first two? . . . Let's try that stork position there, up one leg . . . Now position number two . . . number one again . . . number three . . .

Now that we're warmed up, let's look at the way this game works. The plums will huddle together and the peaches will huddle together and the strawberries will huddle together, and each group will decide on one of our three positions that

they want to do. Then we'll get back into our three lines, in neutral position, and on a given count we'll reveal our positions. **The object of this game is for all three teams to be doing the same position at the same time, without ever talking to each other. So you want to tune into the "psychic energy" from the other two teams, figure out what they're going to do, and do the same thing. Okay, you'll have thirty seconds to huddle with your team and choose one position that your whole team will take . . .**

Let's all start in neutral position, and on the count of "molasses!" show your positions. Ready: Sugar, honey, saccharin, maple syrup, molasses! . . . Take a look around and see what the other teams are doing . . . Now re-huddle with your team. You can do the same position you just did, or you can change. Remember, the object of this game is for all three teams to be doing the same thing as quickly as possible . . .

Okay, who wants to count us off? What's your name? ("Fritz.") What's the count going to be, Fritz? ("On telephone pole.") ("Pogo stick . . . rocketship . . . telephone pole!!")

**Comments:** This game works best with no more than 50 players (or else the team huddles can really get out of hand!) THREE POSITIONS is a good example of the way in which a competitive game can be transformed into a collaborative game. It is based on an Argentinian group game called "El Tigre, El Hombre y El Fusil," which is similar to the game "Rock, Scissors, Paper." (Each team chooses one of the three: rock beats the scissors, scissors beats the paper, paper beats the rock. The first team to score three points is the winner.) Our object, of course, is that *everyone* will be on the winning team!

There are two features about THREE POSITIONS that we particularly like. The first is that the players get to invent their own positions, rather than being told "Rock is like this," or "Tigre is like that." The second is the special counting systems that the players are encouraged to invent — and wonderful new ones are always being invented! Most players assume that "One . . . two . . . three!" is the only way to count off. But counting off itself can certainly be a playful and a creative experience. There's no part of a game — including giving the instructions — that isn't fun to play around with!!!

Trainers find both the intra-team and the inter-team dynamics in THREE POSITIONS fruitful areas for study.

Teammates on each of the three teams usually develop a feeling of closeness as a result of their group decision-making process. And because the teams only have thirty seconds or so in which to reach group consensus on which of the three positions they are going to choose each time, the leadership and decision-making process of the group is usually very apparent. After the frenzy and excitement of the game itself has concluded, the group leader can help the group members study their behavior in THREE POSITIONS as a reflection of their individual decision-making styles. Some useful process questions might include:

1. What methods did your group use to reach its decision each time?

2. On a scale from one to ten (ten = most influential) rate your own personal influence on the group's decision-making.

3. Were there one, two, or more "leaders" in your group? How were they chosen? What characteristics of these individuals enabled them to gain leadership in the group?

4. Were there any specific instances in which you disagreed with the group's choice of a position? Did you vocalize your objection? Why, or why not?

5. Was your behavior during this game typical of your leadership style in other situations? What are some similarities and some differences?

6. Did you have any overall strategy for meeting the objectives of this game? If so, what was it? Did you share this strategy with your teammates?

And so on. The inter-team dynamics are often worth commenting on as well. Although this game requires a cooperative group effort, many players have difficulty giving up their competitive conditioning, and this is worth noting to the group as a whole. If two of the groups have chosen position number one, and the third group chooses position number three, it is not uncommon for the first two groups to make disparaging remarks about the third group, and to make that team feel like the "loser." Or, in the same situation, the opposite dynamic might occur: team number three might decide to continue repeating position number three over and over again until the other two teams have no choice but to "come around," switching to position number three in order to fulfill the goals of the game. Such situations become very interesting for the group to "process" in general discussion: Do the first two teams have any resentments or hostile feeling towards group three for its manipulative strategy? Was group three innocently trying to present itself as a "fixed pole" about which the whole game could revolve for the mutual benefit of all three teams? Or was group three attempting to set up a competitive situation from which it would emerge as the "winner" at the other teams' expense? The answers to these and similar considerations can have long-reaching implications for an organizational task-group that is trying to work together. A game like THREE POSITIONS can assist the players/workers in taking a closer look at the ways in which they are able to interact cooperatively together.

# stop and go

Directions to the Players: **Let's all start milling around the space, walking any which way. Keep on walking until someone calls out ''Stop!'' at which point we all freeze exactly where we are until someone else calls out ''Go!,'' whereupon we start walking again until the next person calls out ''Stop!'' Anybody can call out either of those two commands at any time. Okay, ''Go!''**

**Comments:** This simple game is a good one for introducing the concept of participant control of the game. After introducing the rules, the facilitator becomes a player with no more power than the other players, and it is up to the interaction of the group as a whole to make the game work. STOP AND GO is an especially good lead-in to TOUCH BLUE (next). It's also a good warm-up to get the energy flowing near the beginning of a play session, after some more quiet introductory activities like PLEASANT MEMORIES OF CHILDHOOD PLAY (Chapter 5).

# five changes

Directions to the Players: **I'd like each of you to find a partner who is wearing the same number of rings as you are . . . Once you've found each other, sit back-to-back . . . . Now, without turning around, I'd like each of you to take the next two minutes to change five things about your appearance. Go! . . .(TWEET!) Time's up! Okay, now turn around, and see if you can identify the five changes your partner made — you have a couple of minutes to do this.   By the way, be sure not to un-change the changes you've made . . . .**

**It's now time for part two. Let's hit the flip side again — turn around back-to-back . . . You have two more minutes to change seven** *additional* **things about yourself — go! . . .**

**Okay, two minutes are up! Flip back around now, and see if you can identify the seven new changes your partner has made . . .** Comments: This game can serve many purposes. Sometimes, we've used it simply to sharpen perceptual and observational skills. At other times, we use it as a nonsensical ice-breaker. It's also possible to employ this game as a change simulation, in which the players can gain insights into the processes of individual and organizational change (for this purpose, we'll have the players process their experience through journal reflections, pair-sharing, and whole-group discussion. For a model of this type of processing, see ''Directions to the Players'' in OPEN FIST SIMULATION).

This game has been a powerful tool to help people believe more in themselves. It is not uncommon for players at first to balk at the directions (''You must be kidding — I can't change five things about my appearance,'' ''W-h-a-a-a-a-t . . . change seven more things — I'm almost down to the bare essentials!''). But, by observing how others go about this task, and even by collaborating with others (e.g. exchanging glasses, shoes, watches, etc.), the players come to realize that, in fact, there are an endless number of changes they can make by adding to themselves, rather than by taking away.

In addition to stimulating important learnings about oneself and the process of change, this game is often incredibly hilarious (as people let their hair down . . . sometimes literally).

Pamela Kekich has added an interesting twist to this game. After the partners have made their changes, rather than having them share verbally the changes they notice in their partners, she asks them to take turns back and forth pantomiming the changes that their partners have made in their appearance.

Ken Blanchard and Bob Sinclair provided the seed for this activity.

# touch blue

Directions to the Players: **This game is called TOUCH BLUE, and it has two commands that anyone can give. The first is to touch something on another person — like ''Touch blue!'' So everybody try that — touch something blue on another person. Even if you're wearing blue and somebody is touching you, touch something blue on somebody else . . . Stay frozen in that touching position until someone else comes up here and blows the slide-whistle (or whatever else you've dreamed up to get people's attention) and calls out a way to move around, like ''Walk!'' Then stop touching blue and walk around until someone else comes up and blows the whistle and calls out something else to touch, like ''Touch a head!''**

**Now, when you blow the whistle, think carefully about what you're going to say before you say it. Remember that the idea is not to make things hard for each other but to create a supportive, shared experience for each other — so call out things that people will want to do. ''Turn somersaults and take a bite out of the grass!'' is a way to move around, but it's not something people are going to be excited about doing. And think about the touching commands too — there are some parts of the body that some people won't want to have touched, so be aware of that.**

**Anyone can call out the commands, and**

**we'll alternate back and forth between a touching command and a movement command. One last thing before we begin — how is this game going to end? If you want to end the game, come up, blow the whistle, and say, ''Touch blue!'' Then we'll all touch blue and that will be the end of the game. Okay, ''Walk backwards!''**

**. . .**

170

**Comments:** TOUCH BLUE is the paradigm of a leaderless game, with the leadership responsibility alternating back and forth between the players. ELBOW FRUIT HOP and THE CARGO CULT, which follow in this chapter, are also leaderless games in that sense.

Setting up an ending for a game is an important and an often neglected part of game creation. Sometimes it is up to the leader to end the game and move on, and sometimes (as in this game) the duration of the game is up to the participants. The contract that the leader can make with the participants is: ''We are forming a community of supportive players together, and as soon as a given game is no longer fun for you, you should take the responsibility to end the game so the community can move on to another one.''

The reality of the situation is that there is a practically limitless number of games that a group can play, and only a limited time in which to play them. So no one game needs to be treasured and squeezed dry — just move on to another one!

There are numerous formulas that can be invented for ending a game. Sometimes one person can end it, sometimes a group of five, sometimes it needs to be unanimous. Pamela Kekich invented an ending for TOUCH BLUE that helps focus the players' attention on each other during the game; this ending works best if there are thirty players or fewer:

''If you want to end TOUCH BLUE at any point, stay frozen in the touching position even after the next movement commands are called. When we notice that three people are frozen, we'll all freeze, and that will be the end of the game.''

By the way, one way to escalate the frenzy in this game is to have the participants carry out the touching and movement commands simultaneously (e.g. ''touch denim *and* hop,'' ''touch belts *and* walk backwards,'' ''touch shoulders *and* massage'')!

# elbow fruit hop

Directions to the Players: **The name of this game is ELBOW FRUIT HOP, and that name gives you a clue as to how it's played. Any one of us can come up here and blow this whistle and then name three things. The first is a part of the body for us to touch (like "elbow"), the second is a category from which we can each choose one item (like "fruit" or "cars" or "kinds of eggs") and the third is a way for us to move around (like "hop" or "walk backwards"). So, for example, if I called out "Bellybutton\*\*Television Show\*\*Skip," we would all skip around touching our bellybuttons and calling out the name of a television show, until someone else came over here and blew the whistle and called out, for example, "Nose\*\*Animal\*\*Shuffle." When you're tired of this game and want to move on to the next one, the way to do that is by blowing the whistle and calling out the name of the game, "Elbow Fruit Hop!," which will be the end of the game for everybody.**

Comments: This is another brainchild of Pamela Kekich. It's an excellent way to get people moving around creatively and meeting each other in a lighthearted way (it's hard to be serious with someone holding her ears and calling out "Spaghetti!" in response to your cry of "Linguini!" as both of you hop by each other). Because this game also emphasizes shared leadership (in that the commands come from the participants rather than from a leader), the more tuned-in the participants are to each other, the better this game will flow.

# the cargo cult

Directions to the Players: **Let's get together into one big circle.**

Cargo cults first arose during the Second World War, on islands in the South Pacific that had never had contact with modern technological civilization. All of a sudden, the people on these islands were in the middle of the World War, and planes were flying around overhead, and on occasion one would crash-land on an island. The people who lived on these islands were obviously amazed — they thought that this thing crashing down from the skies was some sort of gift from the heavens. After a couple of days they would go over to the charred wreckage and pull out the cargo that was left intact, and begin to set up shrines for that cargo and to worship it as holy objects. And these groups of people coming together to organize rituals of worship around this cargo were known as Cargo Cults.

Imagine that the time is the present, and we are all members of a cargo cult on a remote island in the South Pacific. In 1944, a planeload full of shoes crash-landed on our island, and since then shoes have been a sacred object of worship in our culture. This is the most sacred day of the year, and all the most important members of our society are here to partake in this ritual. Everyone here has been *invited* here, *except for you.* You *sneaked* in, and your

job during this whole ritual is to do what everybody else does, and to blend in so that nobody knows that you don't know what you're doing here.

Now, you do know a few things about this ritual. You know that most of it — and maybe even all of it — takes place in this circle, and you also know about the sacred words A-A-A and E-E-E. It so happens that all of the shoes in the cargo of the plane that crashed landed on our island were size triple A and triple E. So "AAA" and "EEE" have become very sacred words for us. The cargo cult ritual starts with the famous chant of AAAAAAA. So let's all try that together ("AAAAAAA..."). You also know that the ritual ends with the equally famous chant of E! E! E! E! Let's try that together ("E!E!E!E!"). But you also know that the chant of E!E!E!E! happens more than once in the ritual, and every time you hear that chant you think to yourself, "Aha, is this the end?" And it may or may not be.

Okay, let's get ready to begin. Remember, this is the most important moment of the year, and you want to blend in as best you can. "AAAAAAA! ..."

**Comments:** THE CARGO CULT is actually a very complicated and sophisticated version of follow-the-leader, with the leadership changing all the time.

This game is the ultimate extension of the leaderless game concept that we saw in the two preceeding games in this chapter. In THE CARGO CULT the structure is so flexible that almost anything can and will happen during the course of the game. Because THE CARGO CULT requires the group members to be sensitively tuned-in to each other, it works best after the group has already played together for some time, and it is helpful to schedule it after the group has already played FOUR UP and either TOUCH BLUE or ELBOW FRUIT HOP.

Of course *anything* anyone does can be accepted by the group as a part of the ritual, so when one person clears her throat, and then everyone begins clearing their throats, the results can be hilarious. Centering the ritual on the shoes can also be an excellent focus for the group's attention and creativity: oftentimes groups wind up pounding the ground rhythmically with their shoes, passing their shoes around, or flinging them into the air with abandon!

A process observer should pay careful attention to the fact that at several times during the course of the game a number of people will simultaneously offer options for the group to incorporate into its ritual. Some times several of these options will be taken up at once, and so several rival splinter groups will develop. At other times only one of these ritual movements will become dominant and the entire group will focus on it and make it a major theme of the ritual. What causes the group to accept some things and reject others? How do individuals gain focus in the context of the group ritual? What can the participants do to get focus on themselves in their "real" lives outside of the world of THE CARGO CULT? Do certain of the participants find it easier to be followers than leaders? Leaders than followers? All these are questions that can lead to profitable whole-group discussions.

Games can be very serious business. As presented in this chapter, there are a number of games that can serve as leadership simulations — giving the players a chance to assume and share leadership, giving the players a chance to gather data about their own leadership styles, presenting cooperative leadership models from which to learn. We challenge you to tap your own leadership and creativity — generate your own games and ways of processing them to help people understand and act on their leadership skills.

# 10 endings: when you come to

We try to end a play session so that the closing activity reflects the goals of the session itself: to make playful contact with our playmates and to build a sense of supportive community. Whenever possible, we also like to give the players a chance to verbally appreciate each other, and to share the good feelings they have had about playing together. This process can be a very moving experience for the players — yet without some sort of a structured closing experience, it rarely happens.

All of us have been trained to "criticize" an event — to share with each other what we don't like about it. It is not so easy for us to share our positive feelings about being with each other, because in our culture we're not usually rewarded for doing that. People generally feel shy about spontaneously doing that with each other . . . and yet we all deserve to hear that kind of feedback, and to experience the kind of closeness to the other players that invariably results from such a sharing.

*Competitive play involves comparing our abilities . . . cooperative play involves celebrating our abilities.*

WONDERFUL CIRCLE (the exercise that closes the "sample play session," Chapter 3) is the activity that we most often use to close a play session. The three additional exercises in this chapter are designed to give you some alternatives to the WONDERFUL CIRCLE with a similar upbeat, community-enhancing ending to your play session. Actually, there are a number of other games in this book that you could use as endgames for your sessions. The key is to adapt the structure of a game you like so that the players can share their appreciations of each other as part of the game. IMAGINARY BALL TOSS is an easy example of this kind of transformation — you could simply ask the players to share aloud one thing they liked about the session before tossing their

# the end of a perfect play

object to another player, and you've transformed a name game into an endgame. For a more detailed examination of this process of adapting a game to meet your specific goals, take a look at Chapter 11, "How to Invent Your Own Games."

Games in this chapter are:

**highlights with punctuation**
**massage train**
**wiggle handshake**

# highlights with punctuation

Directions to the Players: **Let's sit together in a tight circle. We're going to share some highlights of our time playing together today. Anyone can begin. Tell us first your name and then share briefly the highlights of this play session for you. When you've finished, give us one of two punctuation marks. The first one is to put both fists under your chin, one under the other. So let's all try that . . . That punctuation mark is the same as a period, and it means "I'm finished and the person on my left should go next."**

**The other punctuation mark is to put your thumbs together under your nose and then wiggle the rest of your fingers. Let's all try that one. . . That punctuation mark means "I'm finished, but before the next person goes let's all change places in the circle as quickly as possible and the person on my left will go."**

**Now it may turn out that after we've all changed places the person on your left has already had a turn. So we need to make up a sign that means "I've already had my turn, and the person on my left should go next." Who has a sign for that? . . . Okay, let's all try that one. The game will be over when we go all around the circle giving the "I've already had my turn" sign.**

**Comments:** Listening to twenty or thirty people in a row tell about their highlights can overload anyone's ability to concentrate, so by the time the last few people get to speak everyone is sitting around with glazed eyeballs. Changing places in the circle is great fun, and can provoke many squeals of laughter — and it also renews people's energy for listening to each other.

On occasion, the players will be so excited by dashing to a new spot in the circle that they won't pay any attention to the person who is sharing his/her highlights. So, with some groups it is important to share in advance the reason for changing places in the circle, and to emphasize that the main point of this activity is to share the highlights.

In general, we are great believers in the proposition that a short break for physical activity can do wonders in renewing the attention span (and make a significant contribution to "retention" of material). That is why a quick break for an "Energizer" (see Chapter 6) can do wonders to perk up a lesson or a lecture (or a conversation)!

With very large groups (say 50-500 persons) HIGHLIGHTS WITH PUNCTUATION becomes too cumbersome and can get out of hand. With that size group, we would recommend ending with a WONDERFUL CIRCLE instead — although the players will still have to speak *very* loudly!

# massage train

Directions to the Players: **Your birthday is a special day, a day in which you are the focus of attention. The only problem is that our un-birthdays far outnumber our birthdays. We can remedy that by playing the following un-birthday game, one in which** *all* **of us will receive some nourishing attention.**

**Our first task is to form a circle in order of our birthdays. Now, my birthday is December 31 — starting to my left in the circle, people with January will start lining up . . . okay, let's see how quickly we can get in order . . .**

**We now have a circle of birthdays. Let's move in so that we're all touching shoulder-to-shoulder with our neighbors on either side . . . Find out the names of the people on either side of you . . . Okay, we're going to turn the circle a quarter turn to the right, so that you're now facing someone's back . . . Let's move the whole circle in towards the center so that everyone can now comfortably rest their hands on the shoulders of the person in front of them . . . Everyone got that? Okay, let's give a gentle but firm back and neck massage to the person in front of us, and at the same time half of our brain is going to be delighting in the massage we're getting from the person behind us . . . If you have any special requests, don't be shy, let the person behind you know what you need**

**. . . If something feels good, you can let them know about that, too — you can let out a couple of Oooooh's and Aaaaaah's now and then . . . Okay, let's drop hands now, reverse our tracks, and have the massage train head in the other direction: return the favor to the person who just gave you a massage . . .**

**Let's move back into our big circle facing inward, holding hands. Imagine that there is a ray of energy extending out from your center, out into the center of this circle, sort of a "psychic umbilical cord." And in the center of this space, there is a spot where your umbilical cord meets up with the umbilical cords of all the other people here, a place where all our energies are merging. In that space, give the other people a gentle psychic massage, caress them and say good-bye to them through your energy-projection. And at the same time, take a look around the circle at the wonderful people you've been playing with here today, and say good-bye in that way too . . .**

Comments: Unfortunately, our society and its institutions often place taboos on touching and many Americans are thus literally out-of-touch with family, friends, and neighbors. Because of these taboos against touching, it would probably be best to hop on the MASSAGE TRAIN only after the members of the group have reached a

high level of comfort with one another. It may be helpful to point out that massaging can be a very gentle and strong way of showing caring, and that it doesn't have to involve sexuality.

People often find a MASSAGE TRAIN to be refreshing at the end of a long day, or when tension is running high. In some families we know, parents and children hop on the massage train every evening after dinner. Teachers of primary school students report that the massage train relieves students' tension, and helps them put their attention to learning.

The MASSAGE TRAIN is, of course, not exactly the best way to give (or to receive!) a massage, but it's not intended to be. It's intended to be a minimum of physical therapy and a maximum of fun-filled physical contact. The last thing in the world you want during this activity is for people to be worried about whether or not they have the proper massage technique. Anything goes, and the more squeals and laughs amidst the sharing and caring, the better!

The MASSAGE TRAIN can be a wonderful way to celebrate your birthday — and all your un-birthdays. In fact, it would be silly for the train to sit in the station 364 days out of each year. All aboard!

Sid Simon got us on the right track by introducing us to the MASSAGE TRAIN. The WONDERFUL CIRCLE, the MASSAGE TRAIN, and HIGHLIGHTS WITH PUNCTUATION all take place in a circle. The reason for that is simple: we want to give the players a chance to look at the group as a whole, and to leave the play session with a final image of the connection and sharing they've had together.

# wiggle handshake

Directions to the Players: **Now it's time to
say good-bye . . . to all our play family . . .
and what better way to do it than with a
ritual we'll all remember: an unforgettable
handshake! Now, for many people, parting
really is sweet sorrow — it can be hard to
say good-bye to people with whom you've
been having fun. The WIGGLE
HANDSHAKE is a great way to take with
you the memories of the good times we've
had together. Can I have a volunteer to
demonstrate the handshake with me? . . .
Okay, Susan come on up and we'll show
everyone how to focus on the sweet part of
parting . . .**
   **The WIGGLE HANDSHAKE consists of
three actions. First, we shake hands
normally . . . then, with our thumbs
interlocked, we rotate our four fingers over
the other person's thumb, grasp their
hand, and shake again . . . finally, with our
thumbs still interlocked, we move our hand
until it is parallel to the ground with the
fingers pointing to the other person — at
this point, just wave good-bye to your
partner, and move on to another person
with whom you can do the WIGGLE
HANDSHAKE. Okay, let's all do it!**

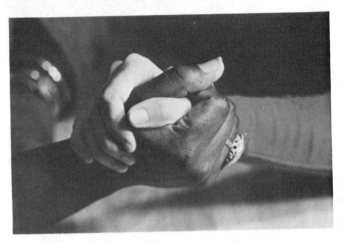

184

**Comments:** This is a light-hearted and innovative way to leave a group of friends and playmates. Many groups we've worked with have used this WIGGLE HANDSHAKE as a "secret code" — when participants meet each other in other situations, they greet one another with a laughter-filled WIGGLE HANDSHAKE. You might want to build on this by encouraging participants to play with traditions or rituals by creating their own way of "saying good-bye" or of "saying hello" or of showing appreciation. We're told that in Tibet people *applaud* by silently holding their hands over their heads and wiggling their hands!

Endings can serve as beginnings . . . The games described in this chapter point out how to build affirmation, laughter, and joy into saying "good-bye" to play partners. These ending games can provide an effective bridge between members until you meet again. If "parting is such sweet sorrow," these games can add a great deal of sweetness and minimize the sorrow!

# 11 how to invent your

There are two ways to invent your own games that we want to take a look at in this chapter. One is to take an old game that doesn't quite work for your purposes and to change it around. You might make some minor revisions in the game or you might totally overhaul the whole thing so that it's completely unrecognizable, depending on how much of the original game is attractive to you. (Obviously *something* in the original game must be attractive to you or you wouldn't bother changing it around!) We call that "recycling an old game" and we'll deal with that first. The second way to invent your own game is to start completely from scratch — figure out what you want to do, put together the component parts, and design an entirely

new game around your concept. We'll take a look at a number of different ways to do that in the second half of the chapter.

## recycling old games

The first question to ask yourself in designing a playful activity with a group is, "What is my goal in offering this game to the group — what kind of interactions do I want to promote with the group?" You might want to make it easy for people to meet each other, to provide a high-energy release, to create an introspective atmosphere, to let the group focus its creative powers on an improvised, whole-group project, or any number of others.

# own games

*I remember playing a combination of jump rope and tag when I was little. It was great how we put two games together and came up with an even more exciting game. This makes me want to think more about how to do this with other games.*

For example, suppose our goals are to increase the feeling of unity and spirit in the group, to have a high-energy physical release, and to increase physical closeness and touching. The next thing we do is to take a look at all the games we know, and see which of them promote any of our goals. And we see that the game of tag can perhaps be modified to serve our purposes.

So we're going to make up a new version of tag. First of all let's see what we like about the old game, what it is that we want to keep. One thing we like is the movement — it's fast-paced and interesting, and the players are in constant motion. In addition, there is some physical touching when a tag occurs. But we'd like to intensify this touch, which is fleeting and actually somewhat hostile, since its purpose is to pass the dreaded ''It'' from one player to another. We'd like to make the touch into something more friendly and long-lasting. And lastly the sense of herd-like movement, of belonging to a large mass of people trying to escape the ''It,'' is a feature we'd like to keep. But there's not really a ''sense of unity'' in the usual game of tag. Because everyone is moving away from the ''It,'' there never really is time to feel a part of the group — it's more like a large collection of individuals all moving through the same space at the same time, all trying to escape from the same thing, but no one really feeling connected to the others. So that part is going to need some reworking.

Now, what is it that we don't like about tag? What are the things that we want to change or eliminate? Most obvious is that

187

it's a highly competitive game whose object is to avoid being tagged at all costs, and so the more agile and quicker-moving players have an advantage over the slower-moving ones. The pariah-like figure of the "It" is an unappetizing feature as well, isolated from (and often taunted by!) the rest of the group. The fact that the "It" passes from player to player — so that many can suffer in the role, instead of just one person suffering all the time — offers no consolation. Many of us have youthful memories of being a part of a tag game where one unfortunate "It," slower than the rest, staggered about exhausted trying to tag someone, while the rest of the players, emboldened by his/her ineptitude, pranced circles about the victim, verbally tormenting the poor "It."

Now, let's adapt our new version to eliminate the negative elements . . . One way would be to remove the skill differences by having the whole game played in slow motion. This also seems to immediately defuse the game of some of its competitive seriousness. The players, in moving slowly, get time to reflect upon the silliness of the whole thing and don't get caught up in the "life-or-death" tension of escape and capture. Because the tempo is slowed down, the players can view all of the action at once, and thus become both participants and spectators at the same time. Everybody looks equally funny "running around" in slow motion, trying to keep from falling over. People sure laugh a lot more in slow-motion tag than they do in regular tag!

Now that everyone is moving at the same speed, it is much easier to pass the "It" from player to player. But we are still left with the concept of "It" as an undesirable position in the game. However, this is a problem that can be easily solved when we closely examine the underlying assumption on which it is based. Everybody knows that it's bad to be "It," that the first thing to do when the game of tag is announced is to call out "Not It!" But why is it *bad* to be "It"? There is nothing intrinsically wrong with being "It," of course, but no one ever gets to find that out because of all the peer pressure to get rid of "It" as quickly as possible. The greatest possible embarrassment in a game of tag is to be "It" for a long time. But wait a minute — being "It" could be *fun*! "It" has all the power to control the game. Envision this scene: if I am "It" I can chase a whole mob of people anywhere around the room for as long as I want to. What power! What magnificence!

So the important thing to be changed, then, is merely the participants' *attitude* that it's bad to be "It." And a tag game like BRUSSELS SPROUTS does that very well by allowing the "It" to become stronger and stronger as the game progresses, until "It" totally engulfs the other players and everyone becomes part of the "It." (If you've forgotten how BRUSSELS SPROUTS works, turn back to

Chapter 3 and read all about it, because we're not going to give out any more hints on this page!) As the "It" grows bigger and bigger, the sense of group unity that was lacking in the original tag game begins to develop within the members of the "It." So we have, in fact, completely reversed the groupings of the earlier tag game. This time it is not the people who are fleeing from the "It" that are the group; rather, it is the members of the "It" itself. And that is an important improvement, because it is possible for the members of the "It" to develop a sense of group unity and purpose in working together to capture the other players, whereas that group spirit was not present when the group was merely fleeing from whomever happened to be "It."

So one of our goals, that of increasing the group unity and group spirit, has been realized in changing tag to BRUSSELS SPROUTS. What about our other goals? The high energy physical release was present in the original tag game, and is still present in our revised version. And by having the members of the "It" link up arms together, we've made some definite progress towards increasing the physical closeness and touching in the group.[1]

The process we have just gone through is, in fact, the way in which the original BRUSSELS SPROUTS was invented by Pamela Kekich. The only difference between the BRUSSELS SPROUTS we have just generated and the one that appears in Chapter 3 is that our version

---

[1]The game of AMOEBA TAG fulfills our goals of increasing physical touch even better than does BRUSSELS SPROUTS, mainly because the players get to meet and physically link up with dozens of other players during the course of the game, as their individual amoebas keep growing and subdividing. AMOEBA TAG is in actuality an offshoot of BRUSSELS SPROUTS, and the way in which it came about is of some interest — it was invented by forgetting! At one of the earliest PLAYFAIRS, a group of teachers and therapists from Connecticut played BRUSSELS SPROUTS. One of these therapists tried later to reconstruct BRUSSELS SPROUTS but he couldn't exactly remember how it worked, so he made up his own version, which he showed to Pamela and Matt a year later. They loved it, modified it a bit, and called it AMOEBA TAG. They played AMOEBA TAG quite a bit with different groups, but once everyone in the game had been amoebafied the game seemed to fizzle out, with all the individual amoebas wandering about without any real focus. The sense of group unity that is present at the end of BRUSSELS SPROUTS with everyone linked together was missing from AMOEBA TAG. Matt finally hit upon the solution for the A!MOE!!BA!!! chant which serves to unify all the players at the end of the experience into one powerful mass of protoplasm. And curiously enough, that Amoeba Chant, which was tacked on as an afterthought, has become the PLAYFAIR trademark. Over the past few years, dozens of colleges and universities have reported that deep-throated cries of A!MOE!!BA!!! have spontaneously broken out in the cafeteria during dinner, or have swept through the dormitories late at night. Amoeba power lives on!

takes place entirely in slow motion, while
Pamela's alternates between slow and fast
motion at the whim of the players. The
reason for this difference is that Pamela
had one additional goal to her game design
that we did not postulate for ours: to give
all of the players ongoing responsibility for
changing the course of the game as it
progressed. (For more examples of this,
see the ''Shared Leadership'' games in
Chapter 9)

Let's take our model for recycling a game and take a look at another example. After playing BIG WIND BLOWS (turn to Chapter 3 and read it over again. We're going to stop writing right now and read it over ourselves — so come on, turn back those pages and read it over! Meet you back here in five minutes.), people often ask the question, "Suppose I don't have a parachute — can I still make this game work?" Sure you can. You've now created a very interesting problem in game design for yourself. You are going to remove one of the principal attractions of this game (lifting and running under the parachute) and are going to adapt the game so it still has vitality for the players. You don't have to worry about choosing your goals or finding a game to adapt, so you can move right on to the third step of our recycling method: identify what it is that you like about the game. For example, here are the things we like about BIG WIND BLOWS:

- The thing we like the most about BIG WIND BLOWS is that all the players have control of the game — anyone can call out categories.

- We also like the running towards the center and the exhuberant squeals as people dodge out of each other's way en route to a new place in the circle.

- We like the opportunity for creativity in inventing new categories. And we like the feeling of lifting the parachute together and chanting "What does the Big Wind Blow?" — the feeling of group unity and tuning into each other in preparation for the unexpected command that will change our relationship to each other.

- We like the idea that although we are members of the large group holding the parachute, there are also lots of small groups of which we are members — white pants wearers, breakfast non-eaters, out-of-towners. While running madly towards the center of the parachute we see all these other dashing forms who are, for the moment, our family — all members of our same sub-group, all declaring with our movement a common interest. There is a bond between us for that moment — hello all you sneaker-wearers: we're all in this together!

- We also like the nonsensical counting-off system where people can call out any three numbers in any sequence.

Now, what don't we like about this game? Nothing. It's perfect. Our pride and

joy. All right, for the sake of argument we'll say that we don't like the parachute, since that's the thing we have to get rid of anyway. And now that you mention it, if we had to pick one thing we don't like about this game, it *is* the parachute. There have been times, staggering through an airport weighted down by two duffle bags crammed full of parachutes, when we've *hated* those parachutes!

In fact, in the early days, PLAYFAIR had lots of equipment. A three-way tug-of-war rope (try to win that one!). Games with a six-foot ball borrowed from the New Games Foundation. A nerf ball that beeped as you passed it along. But we found that in games where we used equipment, the players started paying more attention to the equipment than to the other players. Everybody's attention was on the ball or the rope, instead of on the people next to them. It was fun, but it didn't accomplish our purpose of creating an aware community where people were looking out for each other. So one by one, we abandoned all the equipment. All except for the parachutes.

Yeah. Now, what don't we like about this game? The parachute!

So, the next thing to do is to take away the parachute and see if the game still works. Everybody could pretend that they're holding on to the parachute, and move their hands up in the air while they chant "What Does The Big Wind Blow?", and then put their hands down again after the last person has run across the circle. However, this presents some difficulties. For one thing, how do you explain to a bunch of people who have never held a parachute that you want them to imagine that they're holding onto one? And how do you stop them from feeling self-conscious about holding this imaginary parachute up in the air? Tough problems.

It looks like the parachute is going to be sorely missed. For one thing, it gives the players something to hold on to; and that can be especially important early in a play experience, with a group that is somewhat self-conscious. So what else can the players hold on to? Each other! Let's start with the players in a circle, holding hands. Some one calls out three random numbers, and instead of lifting the parachute up over their heads, the players do something else. What?! Well, what else would be fun for a group of people holding hands in a circle to do together? They could jump up and down at the same time, while moving to their right.

Okay, now we're getting somewhere. How do they know when to stop jumping? Let's say that the last of the three numbers that were called out before we started jumping is the number of jumps that we will take. But we could run into some problems here: what if someone calls out 14-96-557! We'd be jumping all day. So let's make a slight rule change from the

rules of BIG WIND BLOWS: to save wear and tear on the players, the third number called out has to be a number between one and ten, and that's how many jumps we'll take together.

What else can we do? Maybe everyone will get tired of jumping to the right, so let's give the players an option of a movement to the left. So the way the game will work is that someone calls out three numbers (the last of which is between one and ten), then we all jump together to the right. The person who called out the numbers calls out a category, and we all change places in the circle if we fall into that category. Then we readjust our circle to fill in any gaps and then the next person calls out three numbers, and we move to the left for that many jumps.

Hmmm. Let's make it simpler. This way the players always have to remember whether they're moving to the left or the right ("Let's see, we just jumped to the right, didn't we . . . or was it the left . . .?) Let's make it so the person calling out the numbers has the option of calling out the direction of movement, too. So if one person called out "Right 15-46-4!" we'd take four jumps together to the right. And if another person called out "Left 98-97-8!" we would do eight jumps to the left.

Now what about the chant of "What Does The Big Wind Blow?" Do we want to keep it? It does serve a useful function — the chanting together creates a sense of unity in the big group, and lets us tune into each other before we split into our little subdivisions as the categories are called out each time. But it gets harder to do the chant if we're all jumping up and down. In the parachute game the cool breeze created by the parachute moving up and down was taken by many of the players to be the "Big Wind" in question. But what is the meaning of the "Big Wind" in our new version? As long as we're changing the game, let's go all the way — out with the "Big Wind," and in with some new chant. But what? One problem is that sometimes we're taking three jumps, and sometimes we're taking four jumps, and it's hard to synchronize a chant to those different rhythms. But wait a minute — suppose we chant together the number of jumps we're taking together — 1-2-3-4! That way our chant will be different each time, and it will help us coordinate our movements together, if we move on the beat of each number as it is chanted. And when the final number has been called, that will be the signal that it is time to call out the category.

So now we have our new game, CATEGORY CIRCLES, that is quite similar to BIG WIND BLOWS, and that retains all the elements that we like about the parachute game — but without the parachute. Which game is better? Perhaps that can't be answered — they can both stand on their own, and both have their own special attractions.

Now that we've walked you through our system for recycling old games, why don't you go through a practice stroll on your own?

(1) Identify your goals.

(2) Brainstorm a list of all the games you can think of that relate to your goals.

(3) Put a "plus" sign next to the games you feel positively about, and a "minus" sign next to the ones that have negative connotations for you.

(4) Choose one of the games that has a plus sign next to it, a game that you like but one that's not perfect for reaching your goal(s).

(5) What is it that you like about the game?

(6) What is the part of the game you'd like to change? Describe that element here.

(7) Brainstorm a number of ways to re-place that element with something else.

(8) Choose one of your new elements and describe what you like about it and the way that it might fit into the old game.

194

(9) Does the game still work? Is it still fun to play your new way? Are there any more changes that will be necessary because of the element that you've just changed?

(10) Is there anything else from your brainstorm in part 7 that you can incorporate in your new version?

(11) Have you completely recycled this old game so that it meets your standards? Are you excited about your new version? If you are, then why are you still reading this book? Put this down immediately, round up a bunch of your friends, and get out and play!

# starting from scratch, or the itch to invent your own games

Let's suppose that you've defined your goal for the group activity, but you can't seem to modify any of the games you know to realize that goal. Or maybe you can, but just feel like inventing a game anyway. What do you do? Where do you go from here?

Meet "The Morphological Grid." The morphological grid can aid you in tapping your creativity and applying it to designing your own games. It is based on the notion of forcing associations among and between different elements. For instance, Fran Striker, the author of *The Lone Ranger* television series, used a morphological approach in creating stories. He would make a list of ten characters, ten goals people have, ten obstacles that could block goal-achievement, and ten possible story outcomes. Once he had his four columns (with ten elements in each column), he would pick and choose how to combine each element in one column with the elements in the other three columns. A grid containing four ten-element columns yields a potential of 10,000 different stories (there are $10^4$ number of ways of combining the elements in the four columns). If each column contained more elements, or if there were more columns (e.g. setting, date), then the number of possible stories would increase geometrically (for example, five columns with twenty elements in each would yield a potential of 3,200,000 different combinations). The output/input ratio for this approach is incredibly high — ten to fifteen minutes of brainstorming can result in thousands, if not millions, of ideas!

In harnessing the power of the morphological approach to invent games, all we have to do is change the headings on the columns. So, if we were interested in generating new games, we might include such columns (components of games) as:

(1) **Who:** Clearly, *who* is going to play the game should be a primary consideration when you design games. The age of the players, the size of the entire group, the particular background/interests/needs of the players, and physical differences among the players will all affect the nature of the games you develop.

---

*A sense of wonder is a significant element of play for me. I love to play with my imagination.*

---

(2) **Focus:** What is the focus for the players within the game? Unless there is some clearly-defined task on which the players can concentrate their attention, the game will fall flat. The participants' answer to the question "what were you doing during that game?" will reveal the focus of attention. In TRAIN STATION, for example, the focus is to move in slow motion and to be overly receptive to people passing by. In STOP AND GO, it is to synchronize your movements to the shouted commands. In WONDERFUL CIRCLE, it is to share appreciations with the other members of the play community. In this column, you have an opportunity to brainstorm tasks that would catch the players' attention.

(3) **Props:** Most of the games in this book involve no props at all. This is because one of our major goals is to have the players focus on each other, and not on equipment. However, there may be times when using a prop in a game can prop-el the players into having an enjoyable time. For instance, the parachute in BIG WIND BLOWS, the balls in ROLL PLAYING, and the shoes in THE CARGO CULT are examples of effective use of props. There are an endless number of props in this world — a first step for you might be to generate some possible props, and then decide whether/how you could integrate them into your games. Sometimes adding (or taking away) a prop can change the nature of a game entirely.

(4) **Leader Control:** How much control does the facilitator have over the game? There are some games where the facilitator is in complete control the whole time, as in INCORPORATIONS, STANDING OVATION, and TRAIN STATION. Other games have a rigid superstructure, but allow for some individual and group improvisations, as in HOW TO START AN ARGUMENT (the players make up their individual arguments), THREE POSITIONS (the players generate the positions to be used in the game), and SIMULTANEOUS SONGS (the players generate both the topics and the lyrics for their little ditties). And there are some games in which the facilitator becomes a member of the group and has no more influence on the progress of events than anybody else, as in THE

CARGO CULT, TOUCH BLUE, and most of the other leadership games in Chapter 9.

What determines how much control you should retain as facilitator? It depends in part on what you are comfortable with as a group leader, what kind of group you will be working with, and where in a sequence of activities the new game is to be played. For example, if it is the very first activity, you might think twice before assuming that the group will be ready immediately to take over the leadership of the game.

(5) **Energy Level/Size of Groupings:** You will notice that the games in the previous chapters are divided into a number of categories — partner games, large group games, and others. These games range from a contemplative, calm energy level (BOUNCING THE PERSON, PLEASANT MEMORIES OF CHILDHOOD PLAY, NAME CIRCLES) to moderate energy levels (THREE POSITIONS, CLAY-DOUGH, TOUCH BLUE) to boisterous and highly energetic (INCORPORATIONS, STANDING OVATION, EMOTIONAL RELAY RACE). The unique combination of groupings and energy level will create different impacts/effects for your games. Once you have generated a number of possible combinations, you can then choose the one(s) that are most appropriate for your goals and for the group. For instance, there might be times when the group needs a little shot in the arm — you might then create/select a game that would provide for high energy release. Or, perhaps you are working with a group of people who would feel more comfortable at first to interact in small groupings, rather than in the large group — you might then select a calming activity to help them feel more at ease.

(6) **Ending:** How does the game end, anyway? There are many different possibilities, as illustrated in the preceding chapters. Sometimes, the facilitator can end the game when s/he feels it's appropriate for the group to move on (BACK TO BACK DANCING). Sometimes, the game ends when the group has completed its task (1-2-3-4!). Sometimes one person can end the game (WONDERFUL CIRCLE). Other times, a

number of people are needed to end it (some versions of TOUCH BLUE). Or, the entire group may need to reach nonverbal consensus (THE CARGO CULT). In any case, it is important that the players know in advance how the game is going to end.

Once we have filled in this six-column grid, we can then be choosy. That is, we can choose a focus, prop(s), degree of facilitator control, energy level/size of groupings, and way of ending the game that would meet our needs/goals in working with a particular group ("who"). What we have in front of us is a format that invites many creative combinations. Where do we start? Some play leaders will come across a prop that seems like fun, and build a game around it. Other play leaders will first determine the degree of facilitator control with which they feel comfortable. Or, we could begin by selecting the energy level and groupings that seem to fit our goals. Finally, we can begin with the end — that is, select a way to end the game, and then work backward from there.

In short, we have six different potential starting points. In essence, the morphological approach is one that allows for structured freedom — the six columns provide a definite structure which generates thousands of individualized alternative combinations and paths.

On the next page, we present a sample morphological format (feel free to adapt it to suit your needs). What does this grid look like when it's filled in? On the page after that you will find the results of a quick brainstorm by the authors. This six-column, ten-element grid has a possible yield of one million ($10^6$) different games! (That should be enough to keep you busy until the second edition of this book comes out...!)

| | who | props | focus | leader control | group size & energy level | ending |
|-----|-----|-------|-------|----------------|---------------------------|--------|
| 1. | | | | | | |
| 2. | | | | | | |
| 3. | | | | | | |
| 4. | | | | | | |
| 5. | | | | | | |
| 6. | | | | | | |
| 7. | | | | | | |
| 8. | | | | | | |
| 9. | | | | | | |
| 10. | | | | | | |

| | who | props | focus | leader control | group size & energy level | ending |
|---|---|---|---|---|---|---|
| **1.** | group of 10 friends at a party | none | to share your play autobiography | complete control-100% | pairs-contemplative | anyone can end it when they want to |
| **2.** | 3520 college students at new student orientation | telephone book | to learn each other's names while leaping through the air | 90% | pairs- medium energy level | leader ends it |
| **3.** | 300 teachers at an in-service program | parachute | to get blood and people circulating by milling | 80% | pairs- high energy level | 2 people are needed to end the game |
| **4.** | 30 6th grade students in class room | 3 spoons | to make a lot of noise | 70% | small groups-comtemplative | unanamous group decision |
| **5.** | 75 campers aged 8-12 | bag of marshmallows | to laugh a belly laugh | 60% | small groups-medium | time limit |
| **6.** | 25 senior citizens in continuing ed. course | ping pong ball | to create a group dance | 50% | small groups-high | someone says the secret word |
| **7.** | 100 adults & young people at church picnic | a stick | to pretend to take on different roles | 40% | large groups-contemplative | majority vote |
| **8.** | 30 students in p.e. class | pile of leaves | to move in slow motion | 30% | large groups-medium energy | when group task is accomplished |
| **9.** | you and your true love | 10 pillows | to let others know what you appreciate about them nonverbally | 20% | large groups-high energy | when 4 people have frozen in place |
| **10.** | people at a high school graduation ceremony | telephone pole | to hum and make physical contact with others | 10% | humongous group- explosive energy release | when everyone is completely exhausted |

The morphological grid can be an enjoyable game in and of itself — a "game-game," if you will. Brainstorming the elements in each column can generate a great deal of laughter, energy, and creativity. Once you've filled in the blanks, you might practice creating new games serendipitously . . .  Why not take the first six digits of your home phone number, (or social security number), and see what you can put together in the way of a new game. For example, the first six digits of Joel's phone number are 5-8-7-0-8-9. What happens when we take element #5 from column #1, element #8 from column #2, element #7 from column #3, element #10 from column #4, element #8 from column #5, and element #9 from column #6? Looking back over the sample grid, we see that the game generated by Joel's phone number is for 75 campers aged 8-12, that it uses a pile of leaves for a prop, that the focus is to pretend to take on different roles, that the facilitator gives the instructions and then becomes a player in the game, that the energy level is "medium", and that the game ends when four people have frozen in place. Given that randomly-chosen information, let's see what kind of a game we can come up with.[2]

"The name of this game is TURNING OVER A NEW LEAF. Now, campers, in this game, you're going to have a chance to pretend that you are someone else . . . like a famous person from history, or a hero/heroine on television. You'll have a chance to talk with one another in the manner of the person(s) you're pretending to be. It might be fun to see if you can guess to whom you're speaking. Now, when you want to switch — when you want to try out being another person, or when you want to meet another pretend person — then all you do is toss a bunch of leaves up in the air. This lets your partner know that you are ready to move on to find a new partner and/or to become a new pretend person. Some people may want to stick with being the same pretend person for the whole game, while others of us may want to switch personalities each time we switch partners. In any case, the game will be over when four people in the group at one time decide to remain frozen in place, with their leaves in their mouths."

Of course, this is just one possible game that could emerge from the ramdomly selected elements in the six columns. Can you think of another game, given the same six elements? Play around with it . . .

---

[2]For other applications of the morphological approach to creativity, see Joel Goodman and Kenneth Huggins, *The Power Is In The People: A Consumer Education Handbook,* La Mesa, CA; Pennant Educational Materials, 1980.

Okay, are you ready to tackle your own
phone number? Why not try your birthday
on for size? . . . 12-31-38 or 03-28-55 or
_____? What kind of
game could you create with the elements
generated by those numbers?

Are you ready now to grid and bear it?
Why not start from scratch, and create
your own morphological grid . . . in fact,
one of the strengths of this approach is that
it is infinitely recyclable . . . it might be fun
to add to your grid periodically — the more
elements and columns you have, the more
possible combinations and ways to
synthesize original games!

# 12 some answers to your

People really do have some questions and some reservations about non-competitive play. In this chapter, we'll tackle some of the most common and important questions we hear about playing. We hope that our responses to these questions will provide you with some insights on how to take the words from this book and make them part of your life. Feel free to play around with your own responses to these questions . . . ultimately, if we "own" (internalize) our responses, we'll be in a better position to close the mouthtrap, the gap between what we'd like to do and what we're likely to do.

1. **Don't you think it's harmful to teach children about cooperation when the "real world" is so competitive?**
We believe that loving cooperation is the natural way for people to behave with each other, and that the competitive behavior exhibited in the "real world" is learned behavior that can be unlearned. We don't advocate sending children out into the harsh world like lambs to the slaughter,

# questions about play

preaching love and cooperation to an unlistening populace. Rather, we advocate educating children to their own power, to their power to really make a difference in the world. And then supporting them as they go out to help change the world into the kind of place that we all want it to be someday.

The real disservice to our youth is in teaching them to be satisfied with the world as it exists, instead of helping them to form their own personal visions of what the world can be. Individuals of all ages who participate in positive, supportive group experiences like PLAYFAIR come away with a sense of the power that a unified, joyful, playful group of people can radiate together. It is a power that can nourish and support its individual members as they move out into the "real world."

Cooperation is a matter of survival. The real world faces and will continue to face significant problems and crises that can *only* be solved through cooperation. Without the chance to cooperate, we run the risk of having people further polarized, of increasing misunderstanding, and of escalating the probability of mutually destructive conflicts (interpersonal as well as international).

The pendulum these days is stuck on competition. This book aims to give the pendulum a push in the direction of cooperation, so that people will at least have more choice about when to compete and when to cooperate. At present, there really is limited choice — the reward system (e.g. in schools, in business) is often built around competing and beating (the other person). We firmly believe that we can influence the reward systems, so that people can take joy just in playing . . . joy in themselves . . . and joy in their lives.

So, to return to the original question . . . we would rephrase it rhetorically: "Don't you think it's harmful *not* to teach children about cooperation?"

2. **What advice would you give to someone who wants to implement what's in this book, but is working with a competition-oriented group of students/campers/adults?**

We usually don't like to give "advice," and we are suspicious of anyone who says he/she has *the* answer, the cure-all for everything. We acknowledge that this book is not *the* magic wand, even though there are many wand-erful ideas and games between these covers.

But, . . . since you asked . . . we are not surprised that your group is competition-oriented, since that is the dominant mode in our society. Given this reality, it is important first to set some *realistic* expectations and goals for yourself.

Second, it makes sense to us to *gradually* integrate the ideas and games in this book if your group has competition tunnel vision. Perhaps they will begin to "see the light" if you patiently (and persistently) give them tastes of what cooperative, inclusive, and self-enhancing interaction can do for them. Part of the reason why people compete so much is that they have never had much of a chance to *experience* cooperation and its benefits.

This leads to a third clue — rather than just lecturing about the joys of cooperation, try to get your group involved in cooperative endeavors. It could be as simple as having them form task groups to complete a homework assignment, or providing chances for them to play some of the games in this book, or setting up a structure where they could be involved in peer teaching. The cumulative effect of these "little things" really adds up. For students, the medium (the hidden curriculum) really delivers the message.

For "homework", you might want to tackle this assignment: make a list of all the things that go on in your classroom (or camp or office or family) — then, for each one, list some suggestions to yourself as to how you might build in more cooperative efforts.

Having experienced cooperation, people have an alternative to competition. Given a taste of the positive consequences of cooperation, they will be much more receptive to (and may even demand) the cooperative play structures outlined in this book.

3. **Do you have any thoughts on how I can apply the principles and games in this book to my work in the office — I don't think the people there could get into "fun 'n games."**

We really do believe that behaving playfully and cooperatively is a natural way for human beings to relate to each other. We have never encountered *anyone* — no matter how deeply-rooted their initial suspicion and hostility to our PLAYFAIRS may have been — who did not in the end acknowledge that the playful and cooperative part of them was a real and a powerful one. So, no matter how resistant your office-mates may be to the games we present here, deep down inside, you can bet they would love to be playful and cooperative. We know it's sometimes hard to remember that while they're growling at you!

It may take a long time for you to reach through their embarrassment and protective layers, and to make a real, human, connection with that cooperative and playful part of them that has been locked away for so long. (They've probably even forgotten that it's there.)

So don't be too hard on yourself if no one in the office at first "buys" your ideas about playing. This new approach to cooperation is not a "magic wand" — it won't transform people overnight who have only known a competitive way of relating to each other for years. You may need to start slowly, and set intermediate goals as one way of reaching your longer-term hopes.

You may even have to engage in "seed-planting" for awhile . . . dropping ideas here and there about cooperation, self-esteem, having people feeling included. Occasionally, you might suggest that people in the office stop to take time to look at what is going *well*, what people *appreciate* about one another. After a particularly heavy discussion at the office, you might (firmly) suggest that your officemates play a quick game together (FOUR-UP is a good one for this purpose), and then talk to them for a while about the

ways in which playful activities can help clear up some of the problems of tension and overloaded brainwaves around the office. Or after a grueling day at work, when everyone looks as if they could use some additional support, why not gather your co-workers together and share HIGHLIGHTS WITH PUNCTUATION or a WONDERFUL CIRCLE before everyone leaves for the day?

Perhaps you could play around with the idea of having a get-together outside of the office (this might help "free" people from the norms and routines of the office), in which cooperative playing could take place. Hopefully, this kind of playful, cooperative interaction will begin to have repercussions when everyone returns to the office!

We have found that "modeling" is perhaps one of the most effective ways of communicating messages. If you practice what you preach, if you live what you believe about playful, cooperative interactions, then this inevitably will hit home for the people with whom you work — congruence is a powerful motivator and communicator. Playfulness can be very contagious!

4.  **I am a coach in interscholastic sports — a highly competitive field. Can I apply this material to my coaching?**

This is a "Catch-22" question involving the integration of cooperation into a structure that is basically competitive in nature. But it can be done! We'll stimulate your thinking with some real-life examples from a couple of successful coaches.

We've learned (and admired) a lot from Jeff McKay in this area. Here are some of the ideas that Jeff has implemented in coaching college baseball teams:

(a) Usually, making out the starting line-up is a job done automatically — and autocratically — by the coach himself. Jeff, however, has moved toward democraticizing the decision-making process on his teams — the players themselves are responsible for making these kinds of choices. Providing the players with this sort of increasing responsibility helps them become more response-able for their own individual and team play.

(b) During baseball practice, what often happens is that only a few fielders are involved in any one play. And it's not uncommon for the poor ol' right fielder even to fall asleep. Jeff has remedied this by aiming for *inclusion* rather than *exclusion* in his practices. This is simply done by changing the rules: whenever a batter hits the ball, *all 9* fielders must touch the ball before the batter is out. So, while the batter circles the bases as fast as he can, the fielders are whipping the ball around as fast as they can. The net result is that everyone is "on the ball," and everyone feels included. What a simple, but not simplistic, way to develop team-work through team-play!

(c) A major way that Jeff builds

cooperation into his approach is by redefining his role as "coach". By taking more of a facilitative role than an authoritative one, Jeff gives his players the room they need to set their own standards of excellence (what we like to call an "internal locus of evaluation"). The focus then moves from *proving* (to the coach that you should be in the line-up) to *improving* (setting your own goals, playing your best individually to reach these goals, and working cooperatively with teammates to reach the team's goals). With this new focus, winning becomes irrelevant — it really is how you play the game that counts!

For those of you who might be a tad bit skeptical, we think it's important to add that Jeff's approach works! He has been very successful (in traditional terms, his teams have had very high winning percentages) and very effective (his players become self-motivated, and develop high levels of self-confidence, a sense of connection and team-ness, and feelings of self-competence as they achieve their goals).

Teresa Martin is another successful coach who has impressed us with her philosophy and practice in the public school setting. We'd like to share some of her outtasight insights with you:

(d) Many times, at the end of a game, teams will give a cheer by rote—"2-4-6-8, who do we appreciate . . . the other team, the other team, yea!" Sad to say, most of the time, this cheer is delivered with little meaning or thoughtfulness. Teresa did something about this, and in the process, built in a wonderful structure for developing esteem/confidence in her players, and connectedness with others (the other team). At the end of a game, the captain of each team takes time to validate/appreciate her "opponents" — their skills, strengths, and positive qualities. In essence, each captain lets the other team know what they enjoy about them. What a wonderful, mutual, caring way to put people before the game!

(e) Put-downs are not allowed in Teresa's gym classes either . . . killer phrases (in the form of "razzing" the opposition) are outlawed. This has the effect of the players being able to concentrate on the joy of playing itself, rather than focusing on uttering a barrage of put-downs. What a difference this can make — playing with, rather than against other human beings!

(f) Teresa also takes a pro-active approach to helping her students become "good sports." She is able to increase their thought-fullness as players by having them think about such questions as:

Which of these sports in your opinion will put you in the best shape:
- ☐ volleyball          ☐ swimming
- ☐ skateboarding    ☐ jogging?

Which of these sports would you be most likely to do in your leisure time?
- ☐ bicycling
- ☐ tennis
- ☐ fishing
- ☐ skateboarding?

What is the best quality of a gym teacher (or play-leader)?
- ☐ fairness
- ☐ athletic skill
- ☐ muscular build
- ☐ intelligence?

Which would you prefer:
- ☐ watching an Olympic competition on television
- ☐ going to watch a local boxing match
- ☐ speaking to a local sportscaster
- ☐ playing basketball with friends?

Student athletes who tackle the above kinds of values questions about playing are in a better position to make conscious choices about how to make their playing more value-able (more on this in Chapter 13).

5. **What are the most important characteristics of a play facilitator?**

First and foremost, a play facilitator must be playful him/herself. Playfulness is contagious. If it's fun for you to facilitate a play experience, then you're off to a good start.

It is crucial for the play facilitator to truly *believe in people* to be able to focus on the positive, to have and to convey hope in the ability of people to be together cooperatively and playfully. Many of your playmates will at first be frightened and suspicious of "looking stupid" in public. If you are secure in the knowledge that you have a great gift to give them (you *do*!), then you can help them to get through their fears and to celebrate their playful selves without feeling self-conscious.

A play facilitator must be willing to take the same kinds of risks that the participants take — in other words, the play facilitator plays as well as facilitates. Being a facilitator is not a spectator sport!

A play facilitator is effective when he/she can blend structure (having a planned sequence of games) and flexibility (responding to the emerging needs/interests of the group). The greater the repertoire of games and activities that the play facilitator has at her/his command, the easier it will be to guide the players in the direction of player-control of the play-experience. The more you are sure of your own play-resources, the easier it will be to give them up and to allow the players to take over the structure, since you'll have no investment in "proving your worth" as a play-leader. The best gift you can give yourself as a play-leader is to relax and have as much fun as possible!

6. **What guidelines are there on how to sequence games — how do I know which one to use first, second, third, . . . ?**

The most important ingredient in sequencing games is to be aware of the readiness level of the participants and the risk-level of the games themselves. It then becomes a matter of matching.

In general, it makes psycho-logical sense to us to start off with lower risk, non-threatening games in which everyone can feel free to participate. Games that help us to learn each other's names are a good starting point (see the Mixer Games in Chapter 4). It also makes sense to start with games that are more structured (the facilitator plays a more directive role), and to move toward games that invite more and more creativity/flexibility from the participants. Games like THE CARGO CULT and TOUCH BLUE, for example, that involve risk-taking and shared leadership on the part of the players, can fall flat if you sequence them too early in a play session, before the players feel comfortable enough to actively participate in the leadership of the games.

It is often useful to sequence some partner games near the beginning of a play session so the players can make one-to-one contact with someone whom they can pick out of the crowd for support. PLEASANT MEMORIES OF CHILDHOOD PLAY, THE THIRTY-NINE STEPS, BACK TO BACK DANCING, and THE HUMAN SPRING are all good, low-risk, introductory partner games.

Some games naturally lead into each other, and build on each other for an easy progression. REBOUND is an activity with a complex structure, but it is easily grasped by a group that has first played HOW TO START AN ARGUMENT and CRESCENDO. Moving in slow motion, which is an integral part of BRUSSELS SPROUTS and AMOEBA TAG, is second-nature to a group that has first played TRAIN STATION. An activity like STOP AND GO is a low-risk introduction to shared leadership, and makes it much easier for shy groups to take part in the more high-risk shared leadership games like BIG WIND BLOWS.

A game like TOUCH BLUE involves calling out movement commands and involves some physical touching among the players. If you think your group might have trouble with that activity, then preceding it with GROUPWALK would get them used to different ways of moving around, and THE THIRTY-NINE STEPS would give them some experience with physical contact/intimacy in the "safer" environment of a small-group structure.

Sometimes you might want to have a little self-contained sequence in the midst of your overall plan for the play session. For example, when we work with a group of 300 players, we will on occasion divide the group into ten simultaneously-functioning circles of thirty players each. A

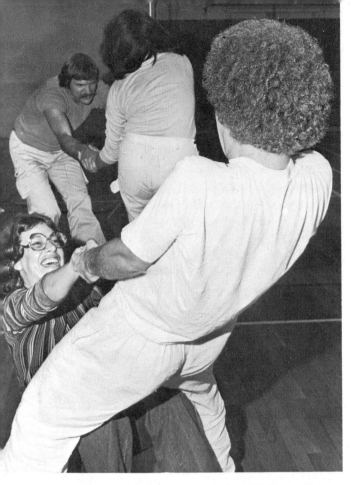

sequence of activities for the thirty players in each circle might be: MASSAGE TRAIN (start off by having the players touch each other and laugh together) ... CATEGORY CIRCLES (this is a sophisticated, shared leadership game, but since this circle-sequence comes in the middle of a play session, the players will have already been introduced to other shared-leadership activities) ... WONDERFUL CIRCLE (gives the players a chance to verbally appreciate the play session now that they are in this relatively small group of thirty,

rather than in the whole group of three-hundred, too large for this activity) ... THE CARGO CULT (the players should be sufficiently tuned-into each other at this point to create this group improvisation together) ... HIGHLIGHTS WITH PUNCTUATION (gives the players a chance to verbally appreciate having played in this small group with each other before we return to the large group as a whole).

We also find that changing the pace is an important consideration in sequencing games. We like to offer a variety of games that vary the pacing, the energy level, and the size of the groups ... playing two straight hours of physically active games is likely to be a good way to end up with a group burnout!

7. **What games in this book do you think are good party games?**

All of 'em, depending on what kind of party it is. The important thing to remember here is that *how* you play the game determines whether it is a "good" party game, or a "good" learning game, or a "good" family game. As long as the focus of the game is on appreciating one another and including one another (rather than making fun of others, and having people feel "left out"), almost any of the games in chapters 3 - 10 could either be used or adapted for a party.

If you're having a cocktail-type party where the focus is on conversation rather than physical activity, some of the activities in the "Mind Games" chapter can get the partygoers stretching their brains in tandem with each other.

Or if your party guests are the boogeying type who like to dance up a storm, how about a party that starts off with some of the partner games in this book — with each guest meeting a new partner for each game? After that's done, let the dancing start, and you'll be delighted to find a relaxed, open, playful, community-minded focus to their dancing!

Many traditional party games that attempt to involve the whole group oftentimes lead to bad feelings because of the competitive nature. For a description of one partygoer's painful experience, take a look at the following anecdote which Pamela Kekich shared with us about her experience of a cutthroat charades game:

I went to a charades party a few weeks ago. Before we actually started playing, I had a chance to talk with three or four of the people who seemed really friendly. We were having very nice interactions. Then we started laying the groundrules for charades, and it just went into a whole evening of tension. There was one man, if I had not spent some time with him beforehand, who would have been hard for me to see as a kind, wonderful person, because he was so cut-throat competitive during the entire evening. He was outraged at anything that might sneak by, that anything might be done that wasn't exactly according to the rules.

It was incredible — husbands and wives, good friends, co-workers were all lashing out at each other. There was no ability on people's parts to see each other as human beings — there was just such antagonism. Then, at the end of the night, after the game was all over, everyone immediately got up to go home and didn't interact with each other at all. It was so clear that there was so much pain involved, and that was supposed to be a fun Saturday night.

The scary thing is that these are all lovely, wonderful people, but the game set up the situation, and people made a commitment at the beginning to play "by the rules." They got carried away by the game, rather than saying "we don't have to play like this, we don't have to act like this." If the game is set up in a way that makes us hate each other, we can *change* that game. But that thought doesn't occur to people — to think that games are anything but sacred." [1]

There are numerous whole-group games in this book that are wonderful party games and leave the partygoers feeling good about each other. THREE POSITIONS, BRUSSELS SPROUTS, TOUCH BLUE, and ROLL PLAYING are just a few that can be great party hits for both adults and young people.

Jerry Ewen, the first Canadian citizen to be a certified PLAYFAIR facilitator, used his skills with group games to enliven his

[1]Quoted in Joel Goodman and Clifford Knapp, *Completing the Environment with People: A Guidebook for Leading Nature and Human Nature Activities* (in press, 1980).

parents' fiftieth wedding anniversary celebration in Saskatoon, Saskatchewan. Jerry devised the following sequence for the seventy-five guests, most of whom were between sixty and eighty years of age:

(1) INCORPORATIONS (for example, ''Get together with two other people who live more than thirty miles away from you''); (2) MASSAGE TRAIN; (3) BIRTHDAYS; (4) INTRODUCTIONS; (5) CHORALE OF THE VOWELS; (6) Singing ''Happy Anniversary'' in five large groups by the SONGS BY SYLLABLES method; (7) STANDING OVATION for Jerry's parents.

The next time you are at a wedding or a Bar Mitzvah or some other variation of a family reunion, take a moment to look around the room and to fantasize what it would be like for you to take the microphone away from the bandleader and to share some of your favorite games from this book with the assembled multitudes. Take a look at your Uncle Bill and your Aunt Marji and imagine what they would look like playing BIRTHDAYS. Think of the atmosphere in the room, and imagine how that might be changed by a fifteen-minute group play session. If that fantasy seems appealing to you, then the very next time you are in that situation, come prepared with a game-plan and . . . go for it!

The use of the self-enhancing, cooperative games in this book could be one way of making your parties sweet and joyous . . . . Part(y)ing no longer has to be such sweet sorrow!

8.  **What about people in my group who are handicapped in some way — how can I be sensitive to people with physical differences in the games we play?**

Bev Ledwith, a dear friend and colleague, has shared the following thoughts with us in response to this question:

(1) Physical differences may be both visible (e.g., missing or twisted limbs, sight impairment, speech impairment) or invisible (such as diabetes, epilepsy, heart condition). A person who looks healthy and strong may have to be very careful about the types of activities that s/he can do. No person should be compelled to explain why s/he does not participate in any play activity, nor need s/he be left out of play or exercise.

(2) Freedom and encouragement for all people to adapt and vary *all* play activities is essential. It provides opportunities for everyone to use her/his creative abilities at the same time that it makes it possible for a person with a physical difference to participate without emphasizing the difference.

(3) The thrusts and purposes of any play activity should be multiple, including fun, exercise of some sort (physical or mental), and a chance to stretch one's skills and enjoyment of play activities.

(4) Only one activity or game for everyone to play becomes a "set" exercise, leaving no choice, except to do it, or be left out. When several activities are planned, everyone has a choice about which ones s/he can participate in. That is oppressive to no one, unless all of the activities are one type (for example, *very* physically active — football, volleyball, jogging), or if they assume that every person is already well-bodied, that discriminates against people who are physically different.

(5) When play activities are planned, they need to include everyone, without discriminating against or for anyone.

9.  **Is this approach to playing successful in developing a sense of community?**

Yes, indeed! Helping to break down the sense of isolation and fragmentation that many people experience has been one of its primary uses. PLAYFAIRS are often specifically designed to help people to connect with one another in caring, playful, and joyous ways. A complete group of strangers can often change into a community of friends within a matter of hours after participating in a PLAYFAIR.

The PLAYFAIR staff works every day during the early fall at college campuses across the country, giving new students a playful introduction to each other and to college life. College and university administrators have been quick to realize the value of a supportive, high-spirited community-building event like PLAYFAIR in providing a structure of easygoing support for the incoming new students. They quickly make new friends and attain a feeling of "belonging" and support that will help carry them through their college experience.

A supportive play environment is an effective way to increase commitment and community among groups that have been working together for a while, as well. We have provided PLAYFAIRS to office staffs and school faculties who have been working together for some time. Playing together noncompetitively often results in a feeling of closeness and support that can continue to grow and grow, as co-workers — perhaps for the first time — have a shared sense of the joyful and playful sides of each other.

Here are some more ideas for you to play around with . . . What would happen if the people in your apartment building/ neighborhood had a chance to participate together in a PLAYFAIR? . . . What would happen if the school year started with students playing together before working together? . . . What would happen if an entire city's population was invited to a massive playful event? (the first PLAYFAIR, for example, was commissioned by the Philadelphia Bicentennial Commission) . . . Our experience shows that people who play together often stay together — as positive, caring, and cooperating friends, neighbors, and family members.

10. **Does this stuff really work with adults?**

YES! It has worked with *thousands* of adults. We have done PLAYFAIRS with college students, staff and faculty members, church groups, office staffs, senior citizens groups, business conventions, parent-teacher associations, and numerous other groups. We have observed a number of significant changes time and again: people who come together as strangers create their own supportive community; people who never saw themselves as "playful" begin to play regularly; people who never participated because they viewed themselves as "not good enough" now feel better about themselves and their own skills/strengths; people begin making creative adaptations/applications of playing to their own lives, families and jobs.

It could be as simple as saying one positive thing to each person in your office each day . . . Or it could be playing get-to-know-you games in the beginning of the semester with a new group of students . . . Or it could be " . . . now saying 'yes' in new situations where I automatically used to say 'no'," as one PLAYFAIR participant wrote to us.

PLAYFAIR participants are able to take their playful group experience and translate it directly into their everyday lives. "We finally got to California" wrote two educators who had played with us on the east coast on the first leg of a camping trip across the county. "We had car trouble all the way across, and got a flat in the middle of nowhere that we had to replace at an outrageous price. We were, in general, having a miserable time. But thanks to our experience at the PLAYFAIR we were able to turn this fiasco into a good time. We realized that we had been playing by the rule of 'we have to get to the West Coast as fast as possible,' and that everything that delayed our trip was making us feel horrible. So we changed the rules of the game and started seeing everything that came along as another challenge and an adventure, and we've been doing fine ever since."

It may appear to be a contradiction at first, but we've found that for adults PLAYING really does WORK!

11. **Are there any problems in running a play session for children and adults at the same time?**

There are a number of potential problems you could encounter. Here are a few:

(1) It is important to be aware of the physical differences between adults and young people — there are some things which adults can do (that young people cannot), and there are some things which young people can do (that adults cannot) — this is important to keep in mind when you select/adapt games to play.

(2) Our culture encourages adults to view play as "childish" — it may be hard at

first to get the adults involved in playing when there are children present. In general, in a mixed group of children and adults, it is more difficult to get the adults to let go of their inhibitions about being "silly" and "playful" than it is in an all-adult group. The adults often try to "take care of" the young people and to make sure that they are having fun, rather than paying attention to the ways in which they (the adults) can have fun. The play facilitator's main task is to remind the adults to stop looking after the children (they'll do fine by themselves!) and to "take care of" their own playful needs! Being playful in public may run counter to the adult players' image of themselves as mature. We find it helpful to point out that the ability to play is one of the most natural/"matural" qualities we have as human beings ... this sometimes helps to interrupt the adults' tendency to be spectators.

(3) Almost everyone has grown up surrounded by a variety of adultist (father/mother/teacher-always-knows-best) attitudes. It is important that this be avoided in mixed-age play groups. In play, we are all equal playmates — the notion of "peerness" is very important. You may find it helpful to lightly/humorously remind the adults that we are all *players*, as one way to help them avoid serving solely in the "coaching"/"I'll teach you" role. In some cases it might even be appropriate to ask all the players to let the young people "coach" themselves (and the adults, as well) — as one way of "playing" with the norms. Sometimes, of course, the opposite extreme can occur, with the young people "showing off" for the adults, and having the attention of the entire group focused on them while the adults stand idly by. This is not a "peer relationship" either, and should be firmly and playfully discouraged.

## 12. Are any of the games particularly good for bringing out the shy people in my group?

Once again, it's the way in which you present the games, rather than the games themselves, that can make the difference for you. In the long run, all the games in this book will be useful for shy players, because the games are designed to create a positive self-image in the players, to create a safe play environment, and to give the players a feeling of belonging to the group.

If you have some players in your group who are particularly shy, who are reluctant to begin playing with the other group members, go slowly with them. In designing your play sequence, concentrate on those activities which will be low-risk for your players (in the "Comments" section following the games we've indicated activities which seem to us to be particularly high-risk ones).

Jeffrey Randall, a Castro Valley (California) psychologist has found the WONDERFUL CIRCLE to be an especially appropriate exercise for use in assertiveness training groups. "This exercise is particularly useful for shy people" he writes us, "because it presents the group members with a positive double-bind that facilitates an assertive response. This works as follows:

The individuals are asked to share their experience of the day while moving together in unison. The circle can stop, take a rest, only when someone shares. Yet this very sharing is something that is difficult for many shy people to do. Shy people very often are more concerned with other people's feelings than their own, and often are concerned with "taking care" of the other group members. In this exercise the way they try to take care of the other group members is to call out "Stop!" in order to give the other group members a rest. But in order to help the group out in this way they must share something about their feelings. This puts them in a positive double-bind of taking care of the group and at the same time asserting themselves through publicly sharing their feelings.''

**13. Do you seriously believe that it is possible to take the spirit of cooperation and playfulness out into the "real world?"**

Not only do we believe it is possible, we know that people *are* doing it all the time. For example, Renata Wack, a West German psychologist, recently told us about the spontaneous formation of a multi-national play community.

Renata arrived in London on New Year's Day intending to take the Laker Skytrain to New York. She found, however, that the plane was sold-out, and that she and 150 other passengers would have to wait twenty four hours for the next day's flight. With the aid of a French student named Sasha and a Parisian entertainer who served as the "Games Captain," Renata was able to turn this potentially disheartening situation into one which all the participants will long remember. While Sasha took care of the logistics of forming a community (organizing the eating and sleeping procedures and keeping track of the list of standby passengers) Renata took care of the emotional needs of the group, counseling anyone who needed her assistance. At the same time the Games Captain provided the entertainment, both by performing himself and by organizing ongoing large-group games.

By the time the plane actually departed, such a strong sense of community had developed among the passengers that no one wanted to sleep on the long transatlantic flight, because everyone knew that once the plane landed in New York the community would disband and they would all go their separate ways. In mid-flight one of the passengers took the flight attendant's microphone and announced that he wanted to make a presentation on behalf of the group. He had taken up a collection the preceeding day, slipped back into London, and used the money to purchase an engraved trophy cup, which he presented to the Games Captain as a gesture of appreciation from the entire play community!

Renata still keeps in touch with her two comrades-in-fun. In listening to her tell the story it was obvious what a special, cherished experience it was for her. And yet the truth is that all of us can have a special experience like that one if we are willing to take the risk of reaching out to other people. Most everyone will want to become part of a playful, high-spirited, supportive community!

# **13** a value-able look at

Our values are the rudders that steer our lives. If we want to avoid a "bum steer," then we need to know what we value. Before we can make meaningful choices about the role of playing in our lives, it is important to take some time to navigate through some of our "play" values.

We would like to share with you four activities designed to help you to examine your values about play.[1] You can tackle these activities by yourself and/or with a group of friends, family, students, and/or colleagues. Feel free to springboard off these questions and activities, to modify them and to create your own.

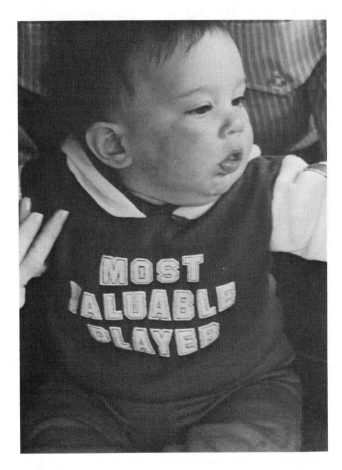

---

[1]For more information on the values clarification approach, see Donald Read, Sidney Simon, and Joel Goodman, *Health Education: The Search for Values,* Englewood Cliffs, NJ: Prentice-Hall, 1977; and Joel Goodman (editor) *Turning Points: New Developments, New Directions in Values Clarification,* Volume I (1978) and Volume II (1979), Creative Resources Press, c/o The National Humanistic Education Center, 110 Spring St., Saratoga Springs, NY 12866.

# play

## are you someone who?

This activity provides you with a checklist, which you can use to identify your own values about "play." It might be an interesting experiment to have a friend (or student or spouse or colleague or playmate) place checks in column A for the items which s/he thinks describe you (*after* you have completed and covered column B) — this feedback may provide you with some good food for thought about how others see you at play.

| | How Someone Else Sees Me<br>A | How I See Myself<br>B | Notes To Myself |
|---|---|---|---|
| Are you someone who...... | | | |
| 1. believes in competition? | | | |
| 2. believes that winning is everything? | | | |
| 3. feels better when you lose than when you win? | | | |
| 4. has ever "let someone else win?" | | | |
| 5. has one "favorite" sport? | | | |

|  | How Someone Else Sees Me<br>A | How I See Myself<br>B | Notes To Myself |
|---|---|---|---|
| 6.  is interested/involved in some non-western forms of physical activity (e.g. t'ai chi)? | | | |
| 7.  never misses Monday night football on tv? | | | |
| 8.  sees yourself more as a "spectator" when it comes to playing? | | | |
| 9.  gets a charge out of fights at hockey games? | | | |
| 10.  ever dreamed of being a star athlete? | | | |
| 11.  thinks that boys and girls should play together on intramural teams? | | | |
| 12.  thinks that boys and girls should play together on interscholastic teams? | | | |
| 13.  thinks that competitive games should be banned from schools? | | | |
| 14.  thinks that your life would have been better if you had been a professional athlete? | | | |
| 15.  has ever been "the goat" in a game? | | | |

| | How Someone Else Sees Me<br>A | How I See Myself<br>B | Notes To Myself |
|---|---|---|---|
| 16. has ever been the "hero/heroine" in a game? | | | |
| 17. only plays games that you are sure you can win? | | | |
| 18. talks about things other than volleyball when you play volleyball? | | | |
| 19. gets to know people better by playing with them? | | | |
| 20. plays less the older you get? | | | |
| 21. still wants to play when you're 65? | | | |
| 22. makes a distinction between "work" and "play" in your life? | | | |
| 23. has said something supportive/appreciative to a friend/colleague/student/family member today? | | | |
| 24. sees vacations as the only legitimate time for you to play? | | | |
| 25. thinks that "most valuable player" awards should be abolished? | | | |

# rank-ordering

Rank orders invite you to prioritize what is important to you. You can complete them alone and/or discuss them with others. A real challenge might be to see if you could reach consensus on your rankings with a group of people. After each rank order, we have provided you with some space to jot down some "I learned" statements and/or to generate additional rank orders which you could present to others (or to yourself). An important thing to remember is that there is no "right" answer to these rank orders — and hence, no "wrong" answer either. As the tennis coach once said, "Different strokes for different folks!"

(1)  Winning is:
____everything
____not everything
____not anything
I Learned...... This makes me think of another rank-order......

(2)  People function best when:
____they work/play cooperatively
____they compete
____they work/play independently
I learned...... This makes me think of......

(3)  Sports in America are:
____salvation
____ruination
____an important safety valve
I learned...... This makes me think of......

(4)  The playing I did in my youth:
____was very important to me in a positive way
____left me scarred
____had no noticeable effect
I learned...... This makes me think of......

(5)  Fighting in professional sports:
____is a natural part of the game
____is a disgraceful model
____is what draws me to the game
I learned...... This makes me think of......

(6)  My life is like the following game:
____hockey
____tetherball
____baseball
I learned...... This makes me think of......

(7)  As a teacher/parent, I feel like:
____an umpire
____a sports announcer
____a player
I learned...... This makes me think of......

(8)  If someone described me as very playful, I would be:
____embarrassed
____flattered
____very playful
I learned...... This makes me think of......

(9) I prefer:
___team sports
___one-on-one competition
___individualized physical activity/
exercise
I learned......This makes me think
of......

(10) A coach:
___should make out the lineup
___should let the players decide
who is going to play
___should make out the lineup by
lot
I learned......This makes me think
of......

(11) A student doesn't want to play
softball — the teacher should:
___make the student play
___let the student sit out
___encourage the student to play
I learned...... This makes me think
of......

(12) Playfulness in adults is:
___something I look for in my
friends
___inappropriate and immature
___something I would like to have
more of
I learned...... This makes me think
of......

(13) "'Tis better to have played and lost
than not to have played at all"—
___I agree with this statement
___I disagree with this statement
___I would qualify this statement in
in the following way:
I learned...... This makes me think
of......

(14) The most important thing in playing
is to be:
___a winner
___a good sport
___someone who gives 100% all the
time
I learned...... This makes me think
of......

(15) A playful response to the above
rank-orders would be:
___to send the authors 15 new
questions
___to skip this question entirely
___to put this book down and go
out and play
I learned...... This makes me think
of......

# alternatives search

Here is a values clarification activity which can aid you in creatively solving real-life values dilemmas. The alternatives search is a vehicle you can use to automatically synthesize convergent and divergent thinking. There are three basic steps to the alternatives search:

(1) Find a problem of interest/concern to you (if it hasn't "found you" first);

(2) Take some time to engage in divergent thinking — brainstorm possible alternative solutions — try to defer judgment on the ideas you generate (don't drive with your brakes on); come up with as many weird, off-beat ideas as you can (it's easier to tame down an idea than it is to think one up); go for quantity of ideas (the quality check will come in step 3 ; piggyback off your own or others' (if you brainstorm in a group) ideas;

(3) Now it's time to put your convergent thinking to the test — go over your list of alternative solutions, and rank-order them according to which ones you think are most helpful/practical/valuable/etc. This alternatives search sequence can be applied to problems related to playing and/or to problems we face in the larger game of life.

(A) What would you do if it was the last game of the season, and your baseball coach had not put you into one game?

| Divergent Thinking (brainstorm) | Convergent Thinking (rank-order) |
|---|---|
| 1. | |
| 2. | |
| 3. | |
| 4. | |
| 5. | |
| 6. | |
| 7. | |
| 8. | |
| 9. | |
| 10. | |

(B) What would you do if it was
the last game of the season,
and the baseball coach had not
put your son/daughter into one
game?

| Divergent Thinking | Convergent Thinking |
|---|---|
| 1. | |
| 2. | |
| 3. | |
| 4. | |
| 5. | |
| 6. | |
| 7. | |
| 8. | |
| 9. | |
| 10. | |

(C) What would you do if the other
people with whom you are
playing always put each other
down after a missed shot?

| Divergent Thinking | Convergent Thinking |
|---|---|
| 1. | |
| 2. | |
| 3. | |
| 4. | |
| 5. | |
| 6. | |
| 7. | |
| 8. | |
| 9. | |
| 10. | |

# clarifying questions

As mentioned in Chapter 2, we developed and conducted a survey to examine people's ideas about and histories of playfulness. The following questions were taken from that survey — feel free to use them and/or to create your own as a way of stimulating thinking about play and attendant values issues:

(1) Describe your most memorable play experience.

(2) Who was your favorite playmate when you were younger? What made this person your favorite? Describe your "ideal" playmate as a young person — what qualities would you have looked for?

(3) Have you ever observed or been a part of another person's negative/painful play experience? What made it negative/painful?

(4) What is a good experience you have had playing as an adult? What made it a positive experience for you?

(5) Can you remember a painful play experience you've had?

(6) What is playful about you?

(7) When are you most playful?

(8) Where are you most playful? What place seems to bring out your playfulness?

(9) With whom are you most playful? How would an observer describe you when you are your most playful What is it about that person(s) that "invites" you to be playful?

(10) How are you most playful? How would an observer describe you when you are your most playful self?

(11) Make a list of some of the games you have played in your lifetime. Spring-boarding off this list, make lists of both the "positive" and "negative" qualities or characteristics of these games.

(12) What is your favorite game, and what is it that you like about this game?

(13) What is your least favorite game? What don't/didn't you like about it?

(14) Complete the following sentence stems as many times as you wish: Playing is ... Playing could be ...

(15) How do you play? Use a metaphor ("play" with words) to describe yourself in this area: I am like a . . . because . . . .

(16) From completing these questions, what did you learn about the nature of play? About the nurture of playfulness? About your own playfulness?

(17) Feel free to add your own question about "play" — and answer it.

"It is dangerous to value what you don't do, and to do what you don't value." This chapter has been designed to help you look at what you value with regard to playing, cooperation, competition, sports. We see this as a first step in being able to act consciously on what you think is important. We encourage you to play with the values issues, questions, and dilemmas presented here — and then to build on your values in taking charge of your own lifestyle and playstyle.

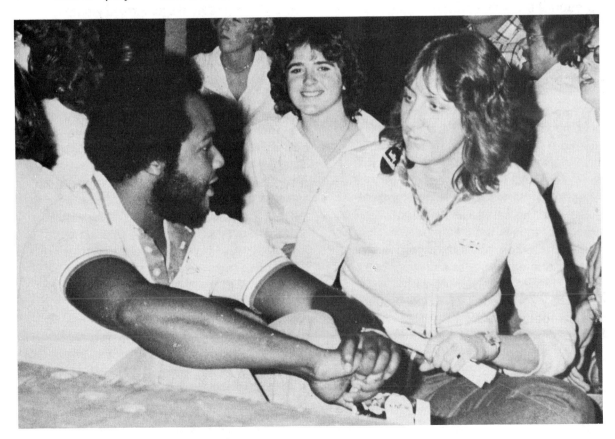

# 14 resources

Our hope is that the preceding 13 chapters have tickled your curiosity and have inspired you to explore further ways of building cooperation into your play and life. This chapter describes different paths you might take from here, including human, programmatic, and written resources.

## joel goodman

Joel Goodman is Project Director at the Sagamore Institute, based in Saratoga Springs, New York, where he coordinates the Professional Development Center, Consultation Services, and The Humor Project. He has served as Assistant Director of the National Humanistic Education Center, has taught graduate and undergraduate courses at a number of universities, and has worked with elementary and secondary school students for a number of years.

Complementing the above activities, Dr. Goodman has been a national consultant, speaker, and workshop leader for schools, businesses, and human service agencies in such areas as: the nature and nurture of humor; values clarification; enhancing self-esteem; creative problem-solving; humanistic curriculum development; leadership training; staff training and team building; organization development; magic as an aid to teaching; creating professional support groups; and cooperative approaches to play.

He has authored or co-authored seven books, including: HEALTH EDUCATION: THE SEARCH FOR VALUES (Prentice-Hall, 1977); TURNING POINTS: NEW DEVELOPMENTS, NEW DIRECTIONS IN VALUES CLARIFICATION* VOLUME I (Creative Resources Press, 1978) and VOLUME II (1979); MAGIC AND THE EDUCATED RABBIT: A (SLEIGHT OF) HANDBOOK FOR TEACHERS, PARENTS, AND GROUP LEADERS (Instructo/McGraw-Hill, 1980); THE

POWER IS IN THE PEOPLE: A CONSUMER EDUCATION HANDBOOK (Pennant, 1980); COMPLETING THE ENVIRONMENT WITH PEOPLE: A GUIDEBOOK FOR LEADING NATURE AND HUMAN NATURE ACTIVITIES (in press, 1980); and PLAYFAIR: EVERYBODY'S GUIDE TO NONCOMPETITIVE PLAY (Impact Publishers, 1980). Joel is presently working on a new book, MAKING SENSE OF HUMOR: LAUGHING FOR LEARNING, HEALING, AND GROWING. In addition, he has written over a score of articles for such national magazines as TODAY'S EDUCATION, LEARNING, NATION'S SCHOOLS, TODAY'S CATHOLIC TEACHER, SCHOLASTIC TEACHER, and A.P.A.'s PERIODICALLY.

Joel brings a great deal of warmth, expertise, and energy to his teaching, group leadership, speaking, writing, and project development. He combines a delightful sense of humor with a serious commitment to the people with whom he works. Joel enjoys having friends over for pot-luck game nights, playing basketball, giving magic shows, getting sent to the punitentiary for playing with words, taking late-night walks, and combining dreaming and doing.

For more information about Joel Goodman's workshops, speeches, and books, contact him through Sagamore Institute, 110 Spring St., Saratoga Springs, New York 12866 (518-587-8770).

# matt weinstein

Matt Weinstein is the co-founder and the current director of PLAYFAIR. On tour much of the year as a "comedian," Matt sees his show as a bridge between the worlds of entertainment and personal growth. "PLAYFAIR really is a *show*" says Matt, "in the sense that it is designed as an entertainment whose primary purpose is to have people laugh a lot and feel good — in short, to be entertained. But one of the main ideas of the show is to help the audience members to get in touch with their own power and creativity as playful beings ("comedians") and to show them that they don't have to be passive and sit back and be entertained. It's a total audience-participation show in the best sense of that concept. Without an active audience, without people making real, genuine, play-filled contact with each other, there is no show.

"So PLAYFAIR certainly is a lot of fun for people, but it also is a show with a message. And that message is clear to everyone — that people can cooperate with each other and behave lovingly and supportively with each other, and that together we have the power to change the world."

Matt is one of the pioneers in the development of noncompetitive play structures in this country. He has an ongoing interest in sharing his expertise with other professionals who are interested in learning about the development and facilitation of supportive, noncompetitive play with their clients, colleagues, and students. In cooperation with Dr. Joel Goodman, Matt does PLAYSHOPS — professional training workshops about noncompetitive play — with staffs of schools, institutions, and business organizations across the country.

For groups interested in a more intensive experience Matt conducts an original two-day motivational workshop entitled "The Leadership Training." He also presents audience-participation lectures to numerous groups across the United States on "How To Live Your Life So It Never Gets Boring" and "How to Run A Meeting So It Never Gets Boring."

Matt can be contacted through New Line Presentations, 853 Broadway, New York, NY 10003, (800) 221-5146.

# PLAYFAIR

PLAYFAIR is an audience participation comedy show that uses noncompetitive games to create a high-spirited feeling of community. A great many of the activities in this book are based on the specially-designed noncompetitive entertainments that are found in PLAYFAIR.

PLAYFAIR was created by Matt Weinstein and Pamela Kekich, and is currently directed by Matt Weinstein. The PLAYFAIR staff works exclusively with groups of adults, and PLAYFAIRS are conducted throughout the United States the year round, primarily at colleges and universities and business conventions, where it is used as "The Ultimate Icebreaker." PLAYFAIR has spearheaded the movement towards cooperative, inclusive, self-enhancing adult play in this country.

A PLAYFAIR is a cross between an entertainment form and a positively-focused personal growth experience. It generally lasts about two hours and can involve hundreds or even thousands of participants at the same time. PLAYFAIR is a joyful, playful, powerful experience whose aim is to give its participants the chance to experience a perfectly cooperative, play-filled society. Participants at a PLAYFAIR spend most of the two hours laughing hysterically in a playworld where total support and positive appreciation of themselves and their playmates are the normal modes of interaction.

The PLAYFAIR staff members believe that they, together with their play-participants, are exploring a model into which the "real world" can eventually evolve (with a great deal of help from people like you!)

For further information about scheduling a PLAYFAIR for your organization, contact New Line Presentations, 853 Broadway, New York, NY 10003, (800) 221-5146.

# sagamore institute

Founded in 1971, Sagamore Institute is a non-profit, tax-exempt conference and resource center devoted to furthering theory, research, and practice in education, in environmental studies, and in the helping professions. Sagamore Institute's programs and services include: (1) sponsoring *workshops* at its home bases in Saratoga Springs and Raquette Lake, New York (week-long workshops in the Summer and weekend workshops in the Spring and Fall at a beautiful conference center in the Adirondack Mountains); (2) sending educational and professional development *materials* (over 600 different books, articles, tapes, films, posters) throughout the United States and abroad through the mail-order Humanistic Education Materials Center; (3) providing *consultation services* to school systems, human service agencies, businesses, and community organizations throughout the world; (4) offering *professional development training* series for the directors and staff of non-profit agencies (e.g., on such topics as preventing burn-out, values clarification, enhancing self-esteem in schools and homes, curriculum development, life skills approach to drug abuse education/prevention, communications skills, training of trainers, grantswriting, creative problem-solving, small-group facilitation skills); (5) coordinating a national network of *professional support groups*; (6) focusing on new approaches to *environmental education*; and (7) *funding innovative projects* that are important to the future of education, the helping professions, and the environment. These programs and services are offered through the Institute's four interdependent centers: (1) The National Humanistic Education Center; (2) The Sagamore Conference Center; (3) The Adirondack Bound Environmental Education Project; and (4) The Professional Development Center.

For more information about Sagamore Institute's resources, services, workshops, and membership program, contact Joel Goodman, Project Director, Sagamore Institute, 110 Spring St., Saratoga Springs, New York, 12866.

# the humor project

Readers of PLAYFAIR might be especially interested in this project directed by Joel Goodman and sponsored by Sagamore Institute. The Humor Project has three major goals: (1) exploring the nature and nurture of humor by helping people learn, practice, and apply *skills* for tapping their own sense of humor; (2) developing and disseminating constructive *applications* of humor that teachers, parents, and helping professionals can integrate into their work and lifestyles; (3) encouraging the use of humor with students, clients, patients, family members, and colleagues as a *tool* to tap creativity, motivate learning, promote health, increase communication, manage stress, and deal with controversial social issues.

The Project provides inservice programs, graduate courses, workshops, speeches, performances, written materials, on-going research, individual consultations on developing one's sense of humor, organizational consulting on the uses of humor in curriculum and audio-visual development, networking, and resource-sharing.

For more information, contact Joel Goodman at the Sagamore Institute address.

# pamela kekich

Pamela Kekich is the co-founder of PLAYFAIR. A brilliant innovator in the designing of noncompetitive play structures, Pamela is represented by numerous games in this book. As an exciting and inspirational PLAYFAIR facilitator, Pamela has communicated her special vision of a cooperative world to hundreds of play-groups across the United States.

A former professional dancer who directed her own company in New York, Pamela currently spends most of her professional life as a movement/dance therapist. She is available to train professionals on a consulting basis in the use of movement as a theraputic and educational tool. Pamela can be contacted through Bill Fritz at the Perrotta Management, 159-00 Riverside Drive West, New York, N.Y. 10032; (212) 781-1249.

# bernie dekoven

# the games preserve (r.i.p.)

Bernie DeKoven founded The Games Preserve, created a number of the games in this book, and coined the terms "play community" and "PLAYFAIR." Bernie is a wealth of information about games and play, and a talented and fun-filled group leader. Although his work as a games designer keeps him from working with playgroups at present, Bernie's book THE WELL PLAYED GAME (Doubleday/Anchor, 1978) is an important one for readers who are interested in further exploring the idea of a "play community."

The Games Preserve was a center for the study of play located on a 25-acre Retreat in eastern Pennsylvania. At one time Matt Weinstein, Pamela Kekich, and Bernie DeKoven were the co-directors of The Games Preserve, and many of the play-structures described in this book were developed during the time of that collaboration.

One day a young woman returned home from a weekend at The Games Preserve and she said to her friends "I just had a fabulous time at a weekend playshop at The Games Preserve."

And they said "The Games Preserve? What's The Games Preserve?"

And she said, "You know, The Games Preserve is the Center for Adult Playfulness in Pennsylvania Dutch Country where they teach people about a new way for groups of adults to play supportively and cooperatively together."

And they said, "Oh, THAT Games Preserve. Why didn't you say so in the first place?"

And she said, "I did."

And they said, "You did not."

And she said, "I did so."

And they said, "Oh yeah? Well if you're so smart, what province in Uruguay is famous for the strip mining of tungsten?"

# the new games foundation

Founded in 1974, the Foundation has done cutting-edge work in the development of innovative, participatory recreation programs for people of all ages. Through its training workshops, newsletter, materials, and giant New Games Tournaments held around the country, the Foundation seeks to help people re-evaluate the role of competition in recreation, change the focus from winning at all costs to playing for the fun of it, and make games fairer, safer, and more interesting for everyone playing. An excellent collection of New Games can be found in THE NEW GAMES BOOK, edited by Andrew Fleugelman (Doubleday/Dolphin, 1975).

We've limited the entries in this "Resources" chapter to people and organizations that we know personally. If you're interested in a further listing of resources, try the NEW GAMES RESOURCE CATALOG, "a playful guide to literature, games equipment, and materials." For further information, contact the New Games Foundation, P.O. Box 7901, San Francisco, California 94120.

# jeffrey mckay

Jeff McKay, Director of Adventure Games, is an innovative teacher, play-leader, and coach. He has developed a creative and thorough integration of humanistic, experiential, and outdoor education in the courses, workshops, inservice sessions, and new games tournaments which he leads across the country. In fact, Jeff is one of the pioneers in the country in bringing together "outward bound" (physical challenges requiring group cooperation) and "inward bound" (helping people to learn more about themselves, their strengths, their values). In addition, as mentioned in Chapter 12, he has created ways of infusing cooperative structures into his college baseball coaching.

For more information about this incredibly creative, down-to-earth, and supportive play leader, contact Jeff at: Adventure Games, c/o New Games Foundation, P.O. Box 7901, San Francisco, CA 94120.

# marta harrison

As a member of the Friends Peace Committee Collective for several years, Marta Harrison has co-led games workshops and numerous Nonviolence and Children Training Seminars for teachers. She is committed to non-hierarchical ways for adults and young people to work and play together.

We heartily recommend her excellent FOR THE FUN OF IT!: SELECTED COOPERATIVE GAMES FOR CHILDREN AND ADULTS, a joyous book which concisely paints the need for and guidelines underlying cooperative play, along with recipes for many delightful games. For information about this book (and the article that was excerpted from it for the August-September 1976 issue of LEARNING Magazine), contact: Nonviolence and Children, Friends Peace Committee, 1515 Cherry Street, Philadelphia, PA 19102.

# re-evaluation counseling

Re-evaluation Counseling is a unique form of peer ''co-counseling'' that teaches people ''how to exchange effective help with each other in order to free themselves from the effects of past distress experiences.'' People who train in Re-evaluation Counseling learn techniques that enable them to counsel each other and to be counseled in return.

The theory on which Re-evaluation Counseling is based ''assumes that everyone is born with tremendous intellectual potential, natural zest and lovingness, but that these qualities have become blocked and obscured in adults as the result of accumulated distress experiences (fear, hurt, loss, pain, anger, embarrassment) which begin early in our lives.'' Co-counselors learn to assist the natural healing of these distress experiences, so that, once freed from the effects of these hurts, ''the basic, loving, cooperative, intelligent, and zestful nature is then free to operate.''

Re-evaluation Counseling is a powerful tool for healing, and one that has had an important effect on both the authors of this book. In addition, its fundamental vision of the nature of human beings has contributed much to our own vision of the way people are and can be.

The excerpts on this page are adapted from PRESENT TIME, the journal of Re-evaluation Counseling. For more information, write: Rational Island Publishers, P.O. Box 2081, Main Office Station, Seattle, Washington 98111.

# clifford knapp

Dr. Cliff Knapp is one of the pioneers in the field of humanizing outdoor education. As Outdoor Education Specialist for the Ridgewood, New Jersey Public Schools and as Co-Director of the National Humanistic Education Center's Human Relations Youth Adventure Camp, Cliff developed many programs based upon cooperative and self-enhancing learning structures. In addition, he has authored many professional articles in the field of environmental education, and has written with Joel Goodman an exciting new book, COMPLETING THE ENVIRONMENT WITH PEOPLE: A GUIDEBOOK FOR LEADING NATURE AND HUMAN NATURE ACTIVITIES. For more information, contact Dr. Knapp, Director of Lorado Taft Field Campus and Chairperson of Outdoor Teacher Education Faculty, Lorado Taft Field Campus, Northern Illinois University, Oregon, Illinois 61061.

# ymca

The YMCA has long been a pioneer in helping youth to focus on the joy of participation in playing. The Y's emphasis has been on experience, rather than on competition. For more information on the national programs developed and implemented by the Y to de-emphasize competition during early childhood years, contact: YMCA, 291 Broadway, New York, New York 10007.

# david and roger johnson

This is a dynamic duo of Professors at the University of Minnesota. David is author of 60 research articles and ten books, including SOCIAL PSYCHOLOGY OF EDUCATION, REACHING OUT, and JOINING TOGETHER. He has extensive experience as a National Training Laboratories Associate, a consultant, group leader, and psychotherapist. Roger has extensive classroom teaching experience and has been actively associated with the areas of inquiry teaching, open education, informal teaching (British style), science education, and ecology. Besides the numerous articles he has written, he is co-author with David, of LEARNING TOGETHER AND ALONE. This book explores how to combine cooperation, competition, and individualization to further basic skills and affective growth.

The Johnson brothers cooperatively offer excellent workshops around the country, entitled COOPERATIVE LEARNING: PRACTICAL STRATEGIES FOR COGNITIVE AND AFFECTIVE GROWTH and A LEADERSHIP WORKSHOP ON THE COOPERATION-COMPETITION-INDIVIDUALIZATION MODEL. For more information about their excellent, research-based, practical workshops and books about cooperation, write the Johnsons at 162 Windsor Lane, New Brighton, Minnesota 55112.

# contact improvisation

Contact Improvisation is an exciting new duet dance form that develops an intense physical cooperation between the two partners. Here are some brief descriptions of the contact experience from two of our favorite teachers.

**Nancy Stark Smith:** ''Contact improvisation is a duet movement form based on the communication between two moving bodies that are in contact. Becoming familiar with the physical laws that govern their movement (gravity, momentum, inertia . . .), the bodies spin, roll, fall and rise in tandem. Within a context of open, alert and active attention, the dancers engage in the spontaneous physical dialogue we have come to call Contact Improvisation.''

**Curt Siddall:** ''Participation in Contact Improv is a study of movement through awareness and a study of awareness through movement. It provides a joyous meeting ground for moving bodies in spontaneous, genuine, un-self-conscious flow as parts of a large whole: two movers, one duet.

To an unaccumstomed eye this activity smacks of rough-housing, love-making, wrestling or martial arts. Actually participants lean to move together on a common path of least resistance in which impulses, weight and momentum are communicated through a point of physical contact that continually rolls around their bodies. Like bolos, fluid and eccentrically weighted, the moving bodies swing, bounce, roll, swim and fly around with a common center of gravity. These skills are developed in non-competitive classes through relaxation and patient physical discipline, in direct association with other movers.''

For further information about Contact Improvisation, contact CONTACT QUARTERLY, Box 297, Stinson Beach, California, 94970.

# inter-action

Inter-Action is an English community arts and experimental theater group that was founded in 1968 by expatriate American theater director Ed Berman. Inter-Action was created ''to stimulate community involvement and to experiment with the uses of creativity,'' and it currently encompasses nine different but interrelated charitable companies and trusts. Berman has devised the ''Inter-Action Game Method'' for group leadership and the development of community arts projects through the use of children's games. Inter-Action encourages Americans to come to London to study with them during their summer training program, held each July. For further information contact the Inter-Action Summer School, 15 Wilkin Street, London NW5, England.

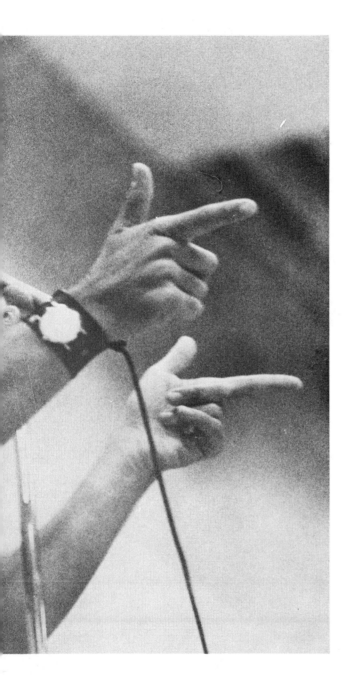

# you

*You* are the greatest resource of all, to yourself and to the people in your family, group, school, workplace, community. If *PLAYFAIR* has warmed you, or made you laugh, or sent you out into the sunshine, or led to a game with your friends, cr helped you make new friends, or in any way brought more fun into your life . . . SHARE IT!

We'd like to hear about your experiences with play, and your ideas for making *Playfair* even better. Feel free to drop us a note in care of the publisher . . . and remember to include us the next time you're sending out invitations to a great party!

Keep on having fun!

# alphabetical index of games

amoeba tag . . . . . . . . . . . . . . . . . . . . . . . . . . . 114
animals. . . . . . . . . . . . . . . . . . . . . . . . . . . . . . . 69

back to back dancing . . . . . . . . . . . . . . . . . . . . 110
big wind blows . . . . . . . . . . . . . . . . . . . . . . . . . 54
birthdays . . . . . . . . . . . . . . . . . . . . . . . . . . . . . . 68
boss, i can't come to work today. . . . . . . . . . . 130
bouncing the person . . . . . . . . . . . . . . . . . . . . . 95
brussels sprouts . . . . . . . . . . . . . . . . . . . . . . . . 50

cargo cult, the . . . . . . . . . . . . . . . . . . . . . . . . . 174
chorale of the vowels . . . . . . . . . . . . . . . . . . . 72
clay-dough . . . . . . . . . . . . . . . . . . . . . . . . . . . . 134
crescendo . . . . . . . . . . . . . . . . . . . . . . . . . . . . . 56

either-or metaphors . . . . . . . . . . . . . . . . . . . . 154
elbow fruit hop . . . . . . . . . . . . . . . . . . . . . . . . 172
emotional relay race. . . . . . . . . . . . . . . . . . . . 136

finger dancing. . . . . . . . . . . . . . . . . . . . . . . . . . 84
five changes. . . . . . . . . . . . . . . . . . . . . . . . . . . 168
floating on the ocean . . . . . . . . . . . . . . . . . . . 96
flying backstretch . . . . . . . . . . . . . . . . . . . . . . . 98
four up . . . . . . . . . . . . . . . . . . . . . . . . . . . . . . . 107

group cheer . . . . . . . . . . . . . . . . . . . . . . . . . . . 120
groupwalk. . . . . . . . . . . . . . . . . . . . . . . . . . . . . 116

highlights with punctuation . . . . . . . . . . . . . . 180
how to start an argument . . . . . . . . . . . . . . . 90
hum-dinger. . . . . . . . . . . . . . . . . . . . . . . . . . . . 70
human spring . . . . . . . . . . . . . . . . . . . . . . . . . . 46
human tableaux . . . . . . . . . . . . . . . . . . . . . . . 138
human treasure hunt . . . . . . . . . . . . . . . . . . . 73

i love ya honey, but i just can't
    make ya smile . . . . . . . . . . . . . . . . . . . . . . 102
imaginary ball toss. . . . . . . . . . . . . . . . . . . . . . 42
incorporations . . . . . . . . . . . . . . . . . . . . . . . . . 40

introductions . . . . . . . . . . . . . . . . . . . . . . . . . . 64
massage train . . . . . . . . . . . . . . . . . . . . . . . . . 182
mind reading . . . . . . . . . . . . . . . . . . . . . . . . . . 150
mind stretchers . . . . . . . . . . . . . . . . . . . . . . . . 156
moonwalk . . . . . . . . . . . . . . . . . . . . . . . . . . . . . 44
moving name game . . . . . . . . . . . . . . . . . . . . . 65
mutual storytelling. . . . . . . . . . . . . . . . . . . . . . 142

name circles . . . . . . . . . . . . . . . . . . . . . . . . . . . 153

octopus massage . . . . . . . . . . . . . . . . . . . . . . 100
off balance . . . . . . . . . . . . . . . . . . . . . . . . . . . . 48
1-2-3-4! . . . . . . . . . . . . . . . . . . . . . . . . . . . . . . . 128
open fist simulation. . . . . . . . . . . . . . . . . . . . . 132

picture charades . . . . . . . . . . . . . . . . . . . . . . . 140
pleasant memories of childhood play. . . . . . . 86
quick shuffle. . . . . . . . . . . . . . . . . . . . . . . . . . . 128

rebound. . . . . . . . . . . . . . . . . . . . . . . . . . . . . . . 92
roll playing. . . . . . . . . . . . . . . . . . . . . . . . . . . . 117

safari. . . . . . . . . . . . . . . . . . . . . . . . . . . . . . . . . 146
simultaneous songs. . . . . . . . . . . . . . . . . . . . . 118
singing name game . . . . . . . . . . . . . . . . . . . . . 67
songs by syllables . . . . . . . . . . . . . . . . . . . . . . 94
standing ovation . . . . . . . . . . . . . . . . . . . . . . . 52
stop and go. . . . . . . . . . . . . . . . . . . . . . . . . . . 167

thirty nine steps, the . . . . . . . . . . . . . . . . . . . 108
three positions. . . . . . . . . . . . . . . . . . . . . . . . . 164
touch blue. . . . . . . . . . . . . . . . . . . . . . . . . . . . . 170
train station. . . . . . . . . . . . . . . . . . . . . . . . . . . 112

wiggle handshake . . . . . . . . . . . . . . . . . . . . . . 184
wonderful circle. . . . . . . . . . . . . . . . . . . . . . . . 58
wrist dancing. . . . . . . . . . . . . . . . . . . . . . . . . . 83

# photo credits

**Robert Arey,** Hickory, North Carolina, Pages 45, 90, 91
**Binghamton Press Company, Inc.,** Binghamton, New York, Pages 2, 244-245
**Thomas Carter,** Pleasantville, New York, Pages 3, 6-7, 62, 104, 138, 145, 197, 217
**Jeanie Cochran,** Tempe, Arizona, Pages 14, 19, 27, 37, 85, 89, 181
**Sylvia Cowan-Aronson,** Cambridge, Massachusetts, Pages 55, 192
**Janis Cromer,** Arlington, Virginia, Pages 46, 47, 60, 109, 119, 135, 141, 143, 167, 169, 203, 204, 224
**Ritch Davidson,** Oakland, California, Pages 31, 34, 83, 100, 136, 137, 207
**Joel Goodman,** Saratoga Springs, New York, Pages 86, 93, 103, 129, 184, 220
**Kathy Humphrey,** San Francisco, California, Pages 1, 72, 113, 160
**Ned Jastram,** San Francisco, California, Back Cover (Weinstein)
**Joanna Jeronimo,** Hayward, California, Pages 56-57, 78, 82, 99, 102, 106-107, 155, 190, 227
**Paula Klimek,** Amherst, Massachusetts, Pages 5, 39, 59, 68, 163, 170, 174-175
**William Kroen,** Allison Park, Pennsylvania, Pages 20, 127
**Art Lehman,** Oakland, California, Pages 4, 148, 179
**Patrick Little,** State College, Pennsylvania, Pages 8-9, 111, 122-123
**Dean Pfannenstiel,** Grand Junction, Colorado, Pages 158-159, 231
**PLAYFAIR staff photo,** Pages 41, 55, 69, 124, 173, 192
**Jan Sterrett,** Pittsburgh, Pennsylvania, Pages 49, 53
**Charles West,** Oakland, California, Front Cover and Pages 32, 50, 114, 183, 212, 214
**...and special thanks to all those players included
in this book, including students and staff members at**

- •Community College of Allegheny County
  - •Frostburg State College
  - •Lenoir Rhyne College
  - •Pace University
  - •Pennsylvania State University
  - •University of the Pacific
  - •University of Wyoming
  - •and more!

# ... more books with "IMPACT"

## BEYOND THE POWER STRUGGLE
### Dealing With Conflict in Love and Work
by Susan M. Campbell, Ph.D.

Explores relationship issues from the viewpoint that, "Differences are inevitable, but conflict and struggle are not." Helps expand perspectives on relationships in love and at work. Psychologist Campbell challenges us to see both sides of a conflict by seeing both sides of ourselves. ("Power struggles between people generally mirror the power struggles within themselves.") A creative and thoughtful analysis, accompanied by specific exercises to help relationships grow.
Softcover $7.95                    Book No. 46-1

## NO IS NOT ENOUGH
### Helping Teenagers Avoid Sexual Assault
by Caren Adams, Jennifer Fay and
Jan Loreen-Martin

Guidebook for parents provides proven, realistic strategies to help teens avoid victimization: acquaintance rape, exploitation by adults, touching, influence of media, peer pressures. Includes a primer on what to say and when. Tells how to provide teens with information they need to recognize compromising situations and skills they need to resist pressure.
Softcover $6.95                    Book No. 35-6

## WORKING FOR PEACE: A Handbook of Practical Psychology And Other Tools
Neil Wollman, Ph.D., Editor

Thirty-five chapter collection of guidelines, ideas and suggestions for improving effectiveness of peace work activities for individuals and groups. Written by psychologists and other experts in communication, speech, and political science.
Softcover $9.95                    Book No. 37-2

## MARITAL MYTHS: Two Dozen Mistaken Beliefs That Can Ruin A Marriage [Or Make A Bad One Worse]
by Arnold A. Lazarus, Ph.D.

Twenty-four myths of marriage are exploded by a world-reknowned psychologist/marital therapist who has treated hundreds of relationships in over 25 years of practice. Full of practical examples and guidance for self-help readers who want to improve their own marriages.
Softcover $6.95                    Book No. 51-8

## WHEN MEN ARE PREGNANT
### Needs and Concerns of Expectant Fathers
by Jerrold Lee Shapiro, Ph.D.

The first in-depth guide for men who are "expecting." Based on interviews with over 200 new fathers. Covers the baby decision, stages of pregnancy, physical and emotional factors, childbirth, and the first six weeks of fatherhood.
Softcover $8.95                    Book No. 62-3

## COMMUNITY DREAMS: Ideas for Enriching Neighborhood and Community Life
by Bill Berkowitz, Ph.D.

A unique collection of ideas for enriching neighborhood and community life. Hundreds of fresh, practical suggestions on street life, transportation, housing, festivals, recreation, employment, beautification, families, traditions, skills, food, economic development, energy, health, agencies, support groups, parks, media, workplaces and much more.
Softcover $8.95                    Book No. 29-1

## WHAT DO I DO WHEN...? A Handbook for Parents and Other Beleaguered Adults
by Juliet V. Allen, M.A.

"A parent's hotline in handbook." Ready-reference answers to over 50 childrearing dilemmas. Comprehensive, practical, common-sense solutions that really work. Short on theory, long on practical solutions to crying, fighting, bedwetting, car behavior, self-esteem, shyness, working parents, discipline, and much, much more.
Softcover $7.95                    Book No. 23-2

## TRUST YOURSELF— You Have The Power: A Holistic Handbook for Self-Reliance
by Tony Larsen, D. Min.

Dr. Larsen, teacher, counselor and Unitarian-Universalist minister, demonstrates how each of us has the power to handle our world. This can be done in a completely natural way and depends only upon the power which we already possess.
Softcover $8.95                    Book No. 18-6

## SHOPPER'S GUIDE TO THE MEDICAL MARKETPLACE
by Robert B. Keet, M.D., and
Mary Nelson, M.S.

Answers to your health care questions, and a "map" for finding your way through the maze of physicians, hospitals, clinics, insurance, tests, medications, and other services in the "medical marketplace." Explains technology and procedures. Sample questionnaires and checklists help you get the information you need for good decision making.
Softcover $11.95     8" x 10"     Book No. 52-6

## YOUR PERFECT WRITE: The Manual For Self-Help Writers
by Robert E. Alberti, Ph.D.

Psychologist, publisher, and co-author of 660,000-copy popular psychology book, Your Perfect Right, offers practical advice on writing style, subject matter, organization, working with editors and publishers, financial matters, more. Particularly valuable for human service professionals "translating" behavioral science jargon for popular markets.
Softcover $9.95                    Book No. 40-2

## GETTING APART TOGETHER: The Couple's Guide to a Fair Divorce or Separation
by Martin Kranitz, M.A.

Couples can save time, money, heartache by preparing their own fair settlement before they see an attorney. Procedures for cooperative negotiation of co-parenting, custody, property, support, insurance, finances, taxes. Includes agendas, forms.
Softcover $8.95                    Book No. 58-5